Goodbye, I Love You

Goodbye, I Love You

Carol Lynn Pearson

CFI
Springville, Utah

ISBN 13: 978-1-55517-984-7
ISBN 10: 1-55517-984-3

Published by CFI, an imprint of Cedar Fort, Inc., 2373 W. 700 S., Springville, UT, 84663
Distributed by Cedar Fort, Inc., www.cedarfort.com

Cover design by Nicole Williams
Cover design © 2006 by Lyle Mortimer
Printed in the United States of America

10 9 8 7 6 5 4 3 2 1

Printed on acid-free paper

For Gerald,
who enriched my life beyond telling,
and for Emily, John, Aaron, and Katy
who were the best part of the gift.

Chapter 1

Gerald shone. That's the best way I can describe him. He shone. He was also five feet ten, blond, had blue eyes and a slightly Roman nose, always lamented the fact that his arms and chest were not very muscular, and was considered by everyone except himself to be very handsome. But the best way to describe him is to say that he shone.

When I walked into the party at my friend Bob's apartment after rehearsal that first Friday night, Gerald was in the middle of a story about his six months' basic training at Fort Ord. I found a place to sit on the floor and proceeded to unzip and pull off my leather boots. Then I opened the large carryall bag that on some days housed everything from books to a full day's supply of food. I took out two large, red, fuzzy slippers and put them on my feet. Gerald stopped his story in mid-sentence, looked at the slippers, and laughed.

"What's funny?" I demanded.

"The slippers," he said, slightly embarrassed. "Most people don't wear bedroom slippers—out."

"So? Most people don't have feet that get as cold as mine. And most people didn't find a great buy on red slippers this afternoon."

Gerald smiled and went on with his story. "So poor, dumb Private Luckimbill was the one that got all the jokes

1

played on him. One night some of the guys picked up Luckimbill's mattress—Luckimbill could sleep through practically anything—and they carried him down to the showers, turned the water on full force, and ran. Luckimbill jumped up yelling that it was raining and he was heading for the trenches."

Gerald shook his head while everyone else laughed. "Poor, dumb Luckimbill. I helped him drag his mattress outside so it could dry. He was so mad he was crying. I'll never forget the poor guy standing there in the middle of the night, looking at his mattress and crying."

Storytelling came naturally to Gerald. He radiated enjoyment. When he was talking, his face was animated and his eyes gleamed. And when somebody else was talking, his face stayed animated; he was still participating, still tuned in.

I was fascinated. I sat perfectly still, studying this unusual person. I couldn't quite decide if there was actually more light inside him than in most people or if he just had an unusual way of letting more light out. He seemed not to have the usual protective layers that most people put up between themselves and the outside world.

Gerald certainly was not studying me like I was studying him. What he saw upon an occasional glance my way was a round-faced, ordinary-looking young woman with dark hair, cut in a pixie style. My one claim to beauty was my eyes, an unusually clear blue, with long dark lashes that looked good even without mascara. Perfect strangers have been known to comment on my eyes, but Gerald had not, evidently, noticed my eyes. Just my slippers. As for shining, I didn't have nearly the wattage that Gerald had. I hid a lot. A person had to really work to get to the real me.

"Boy, it's a good thing the Army exists to keep men like Sergeant Saunders off the street," Gerald was saying. "First morning he gets us together and screams at us, 'Are you men?' 'Yes, we're *men!*' he makes us scream back. 'What'd you say?' he screams and spits on the ground. 'You say you're little sissy girls playing with little sissy dolls?' 'No,' we scream back, 'we're *men*.' 'When you through with me, then you be men,' he says. 'My job in this man's Army is to take you little mamas' boys and turn you into killing machines! Do you hear me? Now you say this and you say it loud. "I am a man. I am a killing machine!"' So we scream back, 'I am a man. I am a killing machine!' And every morning we have to scream that until we're hoarse. 'I am a man! I am a killing machine!'"

A shiver passed through me. How dare they? How *dare* they take this beautiful, warm, delightful boy sitting in front of me and send him through a system designed to turn him into a killing machine?

Suddenly I saw myself, on behalf of all mothers and sisters and wives, storming Fort Ord and taking Sergeant Saunders by the throat. "No more!" I shouted. "No more making our men what you think a man ought to be!"

The vividness of my fantasy startled me. But there was something in the gross contrast of Army brutality, which I hardly knew, and this blond brightness before me, which I also hardly knew, that stirred me.

Later that evening I padded over in my red slippers, carrying a bowl full of popcorn, and sat down beside Gerald on the couch.

"Want some?"

"Thanks," he said, taking a handful. "Hey, I *love* your slippers. They're wild!"

"Wild! They look pretty tame to me. Where in the world did *you* come from?"

"Australia. For the last two years."

"Ah, a mission! That explains a lot."

There is a scenario for the life of a faithful Mormon boy, and, as a faithful Mormon girl, I was glad to see that Gerald was following it. When a young man is nineteen, he gives two years of service to the Church as an unpaid missionary, then he completes his education, probably at Brigham Young University, BYU, in Provo, Utah, where he will almost certainly take the next essential step and marry.

Australia. Two years of dark suits and ties and white shirts. No wonder red slippers in public looked pretty wild.

"How was your mission?" I asked.

"Great." Gerald smiled enthusiastically. "Really great. I baptized this wonderful couple, the Menzies. He was blind, and she would walk him to the bus stop to go to work. His sight was restored after a blessing from Apostle Benson . . ."

Gerald was off on another story. He never seemed to run out of stories or of enthusiasm for telling them. And that marvelous warmth! I sat by him as I would by a fire in winter, holding my hands out to the flames.

"I'm going to make a movie about the Menzies one day. What great people." He said it matter-of-factly, like anybody else would say, "I'm going to the store."

"You are?" I asked. "You're going to make movies?"

"You bet!" Gerald grinned. "I'm going to find great stories that teach great lessons, and I'm going to make movies."

Gerald never said, "I wish I could . . ." He always said, "I'm going to . . ." And he said it with such conviction that I believed him. Always.

Rehearsals became even more interesting for me than they had been before the party. We were preparing Thornton Wilder's *The Skin of Our Teeth* for production at BYU. Gerald played the part of the stage manager and I played Mrs. Antrobus. Of the two female parts, I would have much preferred to play Sabina, the sexy one. She was described by the playwright as "straw-blond, over-rouged," while Mrs. Antrobus was described as "a majestic matron." But I was cast as Mrs. Antrobus, and contented myself that it was actually the better part.

I was twenty-five, certainly not yet a matron, majestic or otherwise. But I was definitely a *somebody*. Gerald was terribly impressed by my credentials. I had already graduated from BYU in drama in 1962, got a master's the next year, won BYU's "Best Actress" award two years in a row, traveled with the drama department to perform for the USO in the Orient, and won first place in the campus poetry competition. After BYU I taught for a year at Snow College in Ephraim, Utah, and then I retired to see the world, spending a year in Europe, Greece, Russia, East Africa, and Israel, where I worked on a kibbutz and studied Hebrew. I was now working as a scriptwriter for BYU's motion picture department.

Because he'd taken time off, Gerald was still an undergraduate. Born in Salt Lake City, as I was, he was the eldest of five children. He had begun working full time in a grocery store when he was thirteen, was generally in the middle of whatever pranks were played in high school, and was a knowledgeable musician, talking easily about composers I had never even heard of. And he was crazy about Barbra Streisand.

One night as we were waiting for Dr. Metten to give us his critique of the rehearsal, Gerald sat down in the seat next to me. "You are a really good actress," he said. "I love your speech at the beginning of act two. And my favorite line—"

"Don't tell me," I interrupted. "'The tomato is edible. Can you all hear me? The tomato is edible.'" Every night when I gave that line I had heard a solitary peal of laughter from the darkened theater—Gerald's laugh, unmistakable, uninhibited, and filled with delight.

And now he laughed again.

"How did you know?"

I narrowed my eyes dramatically and leaned in. "I know everything," I said. "And don't you ever forget it."

Gerald nodded seriously. "I'll try not to."

There was no way I could have avoided falling in love with Gerald. Wherever he was I found myself leaning in his direction. I looked forward to our one-minute polka together after the final curtain came down and the music came up. And when our show was over, I frequently dropped in to rehearsals of the next play he was in, *Teahouse of the August Moon,* and went home and wrote in my diary how beautiful he was.

All that was in the spring of 1965. During those same weeks the headlines predicted that 100,000 troops would be sent to Vietnam, Malcolm X was shot and killed, and I sold my first magazine article, a piece on Russian theater to *Playbill,* the New York theater program. But the only thing that really mattered was that I was in love.

And that was precisely the next major step in the scenario that I, as a good Mormon girl, was supposed to follow. I was a fourth-generation Mormon and never questioned that I would live life according to the gospel plan. I knew that I should develop all my talents and learn and grow, and excel in everything I could. That's why I was a straight-A student in high school, was editor of the school paper, president of the Thespian Club, won "superiors" in the state speech and drama meets, and won an oratorical contest that made me Utah's representative at the Alexander Hamilton Bicentennial Constitutional Convention in Philadelphia—even having my picture taken with President Eisenhower in the White House rose garden and appearing on the front page of the New York *Times.* That's why I worked so hard in college to get good grades and achieve in every way. God had an eternity of growing and learning in store for me, and I was determined to get a good start.

But I also knew it was impossible to grow well alone. Ever since the Garden of Eden, man and woman have needed one another. According to Mormon doctrine, no one can reach the highest degree of eternal exaltation as a single person. Here, or in the next world, a proper marriage will have to be made.

When I was growing up, marriage was a favorite theme of our prophet, David O. McKay, a tall, beautiful, white-haired man. I watched him at conference and at devotional and I drank in every word. "The eternity of the marriage covenant," he said, "is a glorious revelation, giving assurance to hearts bound by the golden clasp of love and sealed by authority of the Holy Priesthood that their union is eternal."

That image, planted early and nourished almost daily, was alive within me and was the touchstone by which every decision was made. My own father and mother had been married in the temple, and when my mother died in my fifteenth year I knew that she and my father would be together again, that all of us, my three brothers and my sister and I would be family forever. Of course I wanted an eternal marriage for myself. I would be ready when the time came. I would be sexually pure and worthy to go to the temple, as would the young man who would take me there. We would both be as pure as the rose that was used as a visual aid in the dozens of "Standards Nights" and lessons in Sunday School classes I had attended on the subject of chastity.

I had had a few important relationships in college, but none of them had worked out for marriage. Still, I was doing all the right things. Surely the blessing would come. There was a joke going around BYU that if a girl graduated without getting married, she got her tuition refunded. I had graduated several years ago, but was not getting desperate. I believed implicitly in a Mormon version of the Cinderella story. If you keep yourself worthy and read the scriptures regularly and pray and fast and wear reasonably attractive clothing and keep your hair nice and use deodorant and know how to make great cookies and appear at the right places at the right times—especially Church-sponsored meetings and dances and other socials—your chances for finding your eternal mate are practically assured.

Certainly Gerald felt the pressure to marry even more than I did. A single woman, an "unclaimed jewel," is still acceptable. A single man is not. We had already joked about Brigham Young's statement that "any young man over the age of twenty-one who is not married is a menace to the community." Gerald was serious about his eternal salvation. He would want to do the right thing. I would be patient.

Occasionally in the evening Gerald would walk the few blocks from his apartment to mine to play the piano or just sit and visit. Once he took out a pad of paper and a pencil to write down something I said because it was so wise. That was not really what I had in mind, but I took what I could get.

One day Gerald came rushing over, waving a letter he had just gotten in the mail. "Look! Birthday greetings from Barbra Streisand. 'Happy Days, Always' Did you do this?"

"I cannot tell a lie, Gerald. I did it."

"The note mentioned my girlfriend. And I—well, I don't really have a girlfriend. So I thought maybe you . . ." And he gave me a hug.

That was a little closer to what I had in mind.

A few weeks later I moved into the old family home that my father was selling, which was now vacant. I was only to be there for a month, so I took out of my many boxes just those things necessary to survive.

"Aren't you going to unpack and fix the place up?" Gerald asked the first time he visited me there. "It's so empty. What about all those great things you got in the Orient? And all the African stuff. Take them out. Enjoy them!"

"For one month? I don't want to unpack everything and then pack it all up in a month."

"Carol Lynn." Gerald looked at me firmly. "It's one month of your *life*! Who was it said, 'Your house is your larger self.'

Now, don't you want to have a beautiful larger self?"

I looked at Gerald and nodded. Certainly I did. Of course I did.

I unpacked. I took out the Japanese lamps and the wall hangings and the brass vases and the African drum and masks and ebony figures and fixed up one room in the house quite beautifully. Then I invited Gerald over for a small supper of tacos.

"Wonderful," he said as he surveyed the room. "You now have a terrific larger self. And your smaller self isn't so bad either."

How romantic, I thought, blushing a little as I slid a taco onto a gleaming china plate I had unpacked for the occasion. The taco looked small and ashamed.

"Sorry this is so modest," I said. "Tacos and carrot sticks are about the extent of my culinary talents. I know a *real woman* is never happier than in the kitchen. Guess I'm not one."

"Well, nobody can be everything," said Gerald, generously picking up the taco. "Say, I've been meaning to ask you. How come some of your friends call you Blossom?"

"An old boyfriend named me Magnolia Blossom Jones. Just kind of a silly, private thing, but the 'Blossom' part stuck." I laughed, remembering. "One day a friend sent a letter to Mrs. Magnolia Blossom Jones at our address. Daddy got the mail first, and before I got home he had gone all the way around the block looking for Mrs. Jones."

"Blossom. I like that. It fits. You keep unfolding all the time. Well, Blossom, how about another taco? You are a *real woman.* I mean, these carrot sticks are incredible."

A few weeks later Gerald invited me over to a dinner he and his new roommate, Paul, had been planning. I sat at the table beside Mario and Dana and talked about their recent engagement. They were very much in love and good friends at the same time. I considered them an inspiring example.

When dinner time arrived, Gerald stepped into the

doorway wearing a white apron and carrying a huge, steaming silver tray. With a flourish he put it down in the center of the table. Around the outside of the tray was a circle of buttered spaghetti, and in the middle a large pile of sautéed chunks of chicken breast, purple onions, green and black olives, and a few sprigs of parsley.

All the guests "oohed" their appreciation. "Be still, my heart," said Mario, clutching his chest.

I looked from the tray up to Gerald's beaming face. "It's not much," he said. "The trick is loads of rosemary. I *love* rosemary. And lots of garlic and butter."

My eyes traveled back to the tray. "Gerald," I breathed reverently, "you are a—*real woman!*"

Gerald laughed, and Paul, behind him, turned away in a giant guffaw.

Why did I say that? I thought. *What a dumb thing to say.*

But Gerald was happily dishing up his masterpiece. "No, no. Here. You've got to have more onions. And olives. Here." No wonder my little taco had looked so ashamed.

Midway through the meal Mario turned to me quietly. "Blossom, what are these adoring looks you keep giving the chef?"

I blushed and smiled. "You caught me."

"And how does he feel?"

"He loves me," I whispered back, "like he loves Rosemary, whoever she is. And garlic. And butter."

When Gerald called to ask me to go to a movie at the drive-in, I was elated. When he told me he and his roommate would be by to pick me up at seven, I thought it was a double date. But when we didn't stop for another girl, I realized it was just us three. Okay. Gerald sat between me and Paul, and when the movie filled the screen, he reached over to hold my hand. I couldn't believe it. He had never done such a thing before. I kept my face forward, but my peripheral vision was filled with Gerald. He was enjoying the movie and I was enjoying him. Paul was not enjoying anything.

The light from the screen flickered over their faces. Gerald was alive, as always, absorbed. Paul was—pouting. He was hunched over the steering wheel, glowering. He must wish he had a girl to hold hands with.

Gerald and I passed the summer as good friends, but I began to sense in him a restlessness, something I did not understand, pulling toward me and a drawing away from me at the same time. I knew he wasn't seeing any other girls, but he wasn't really seeing me either. We were just buddies. I wrote a sad, melodramatic song and played it on my guitar on the porch to the gentle summer evenings filled with the smell of roses and new-cut grass. "You love me like you love the sunset . . ."

I was sitting outside one evening, staring at the stars. Gerald hadn't been by for a couple of weeks and I had missed him.

"Hi."

I looked up, startled to see him standing in front of me.

"Well, hi yourself, Gerald," I said. "Where you been all my life?"

He sat down and didn't say anything for a minute or so. "I haven't been over for a while," he said finally. "I've been feeling sort of . . . strange. Sort of . . . obligated, I guess."

"Gerald." I reached over and put a hand on his knee. "The only thing you are obligated to with me is to be honest. That's all I want from you."

"Really?" His face lit up like a little sun. "You mean I don't have to fall in love with you? I can just love you like I do?"

My laugh was a protective reflex. *Dear Gerald. Oh, dear boy. Love me like you love the sunset and ask my permission.*

"Gerald, I think love is wonderful in any form it takes."

"Oh, Blossom, you're so terrific." Were there tears in

Gerald's eyes? "Do you know what I really wish?"

"What?"

"That I would fall madly in love with you and you with me and we would get married and have children and accomplish great things and have a wonderful life." He was silent for a moment, chewing on the end of a little blade of grass. Then he spoke so that I could barely hear him. "That's what I wish."

There was no sound for a few minutes, except for the crickets and the occasional passing of a car. Then Gerald sat up with sudden determination.

"Blossom, this weekend I'm going up to the mountains. I've been thinking about it for months. I'm going to fast and pray and wrestle with the Lord for three days. I need some answers. I've got to get some answers!"

Gerald went up to the mountains. He left Friday afternoon and was to come back sometime on Monday. I decided to fast with him, maybe not for three whole days, but at least for one! I could do that. And pray for him. But that was nothing new. I had been praying for him for a long time.

Saturday morning it started to rain. I watched the lightning and listened to the thunder and prayed harder. "Dear God, give Gerald his answers quick and let him come down. Please!"

I called Gerald's apartment and spoke to Paul. No, Gerald had not come back yet. Paul wasn't really rude to me, just sort of curt, as he'd been since the drive-in movie.

Toward evening the storm lifted, but then set in again in earnest. It must be horrendous up in the mountains, I thought. Please let Gerald have the good sense to come down. About nine in the evening the phone rang.

"Blossom?"

"Gerald, where *are* you?"

"Home. Can I come over?"

"Of course."

Gerald had put on dry clothes, but his hair was still wet. He sat slumped at the kitchen table, slowly stirring his soup, his buoyancy gone for the first time since we met.

"What a weakling," he said in disgust. "I should have stayed up there. I should have had enough faith. I promised myself—I promised the Lord—I would stay up there and fast and pray for three days. What a weakling!"

"Gerald," I reached over and touched his arm. "You are not a weakling. You are a good and a strong man. Moses would not have stayed up there in this storm in just a little sleeping bag. Moses would have caught pneumonia!"

"But why did it have to *storm*? This was so important to me!"

I smiled. "Did you think the Lord would hold back the storm for you?"

Gerald sighed. "I had such faith that this weekend I would make a real breakthrough. There are some things—" Gerald's voice broke with emotion. "Some things I've got to understand . . . I've got to find some answers to."

"Can I help? I want to."

"I don't know," Gerald said softly. "I don't know."

Gerald wasn't anxious to go yet. It was still raining, and Paul would be there by now and would laugh at him. He hadn't wanted Gerald to go up at all. He thought it was ridiculous. I settled Gerald comfortably on the couch, got my guitar, and sang him a lullaby my mother used to sing to me when I was little. Gerald closed his eyes and looked peaceful, almost content. It felt wonderful to comfort him.

When I put down the guitar, Gerald reached out and took my hand.

"Blossom? Come sit with me." Then he smiled. "I promise not to get fresh."

I sighed loudly and sat down close to him. "Well, I'll sit with you anyway."

Gerald put an arm around me and I lay my head on his shoulder.

"Blossom?"

"Gerald?"

"I like you."

"I know."

"Blossom?"

"Hmm?"

"I love you."

"I know."

Like you love the sunset, I thought. *But that's okay, Gerald Pearson. Interesting things are happening. And I'll stick around and see what's next.* I was in the habit of saying little prayers at odd moments, and I said one now. I was thankful for all of my usual things and I blessed all of my usual things. Then I took one of Gerald's hands between both of mine and I blessed him—that whatever storms there were inside of him would be calmed, that he would get all the answers to all his questions, that he would be happy, and that every good thing would be his.

Hardly had I said amen when Gerald's hand traveled to my face and turned me toward him. Then his mouth was on mine. There was just one kiss—one thoroughly satisfying, thoroughly memorable kiss.

"You're so soft," he said, as if surprised. "So soft!"

I pressed my cheek against his chest. Gerald was silent for a moment, and then began to speak with the old enthusiasm. "Blossom! Maybe the storm was my answer. Maybe God sent me off the mountain—to you. Maybe you are my answer!"

Chapter 2

The next day Gerald moved out of his apartment into a new place about six blocks away. Paul was furious. He glowered at us while we were packing Gerald's books and stereo, and then he disappeared. When I asked Gerald about it, he said it couldn't be helped, that he had to move.

And then he threw himself into falling in love with me. He did it beautifully, the way he did everything. He did it enthusiastically, like he was preparing a wonderful dinner. He delighted in it, savored every step, watched wide-eyed as it came together.

I thought the millennium had arrived. Gerald was in love with me, and not the way a man loves a sunset—the way a man loves a woman! There he was, standing at my door with snowflakes in his blond hair and on his blond eyelashes, with a Joan Baez album in his hand, a present squeezed from his slim wages from working in the bakery at BYU. There he was on the telephone, calling just to hear my voice before he went to class. There he was staring at me with a world of hope in his eyes as we sat on my couch holding hands: "You're so neat, Blossom. You are *so* neat!" There he was holding me and kissing me and saying, "I love you." Surely, surely the millennium was here.

About the middle of December, as we were snuggling

on the couch with soft Christmas music in the background, Gerald spoke.

"Blossom? Do you know what I want?"

"What?"

"I want to marry you."

I didn't speak. I played what I had just heard over and over. He had said it. He had actually said it.

"Hello? Are you there?"

"You sound very sure."

"I'm sure. Will you?"

"I want you to be absolutely sure," I said. "You're so impetuous, Gerald. Wonderful, but impetuous. Marriage isn't like that."

"I know, Blossom," Gerald said patiently. "Don't you think I've heard the same talks at Church that you've heard? And read the same scriptures? 'Time and all eternity.' That's how long I want you, Blossom. That's how long I want *us*."

Suddenly the "Hallelujah Chorus" boomed out from my little stereo in the corner. I couldn't contain my laughter. "Hallelujah, Hallelujah, Ha-le-lu-jah." Isn't this what I had been praying for all these months? Of course I would say yes. Of course Gerald knew what he was getting into. Yes, he was impatient and impetuous, but I trusted him completely. If Gerald wanted me, he could have me. For time and all eternity.

On Christmas day we walked around the grounds of the Mormon temple in Salt Lake City, ablaze with lights for the holidays. The modifier in that sentence is just as well left ambiguous; the temple grounds were ablaze, but we were too. In just a few months we would go into that beautiful building to be married. Now I was wearing a small, lovely diamond ring that Gerald had ceremoniously presented, tucked in an intricate pocket of white ribbon in a scrapbook with a lengthy, ecstatic poem.

We had spent Christmas with Gerald's family. His

parents, good hardworking people, had built their home with their own hands. Gerald proudly told me of the day his mother, weary of waiting for the means to hire builders, had taken a shovel and gone out to the lot and started digging. At Christmas dinner Gerald's parents told stories about him when he was little. "This kid could never sit still," laughed his father. "We'd sit at the dinner table and he'd jump down and run around a dozen times before we were through. One time I rigged up a stool so if he didn't sit still and mind his business, it would tip over and he'd end up on the floor. That cured him, all right!"

I could not take Gerald home to meet my parents. My father and stepmother were spending the winter in St. George, Utah, where the climate was milder. They spent their days doing "temple work," important Mormon ordinances performed by proxy on behalf of the dead. But Gerald and I sent Daddy and Gladys a tape recording we made, telling them of our plans to be married. And Gerald wrote them a personal letter.

"Brother Wright," he wrote, "I feel especially inclined to seek your blessings upon the decision Carol Lynn and I have made. I love her very much, and I feel in our relationship the potential of an even greater love than that which we now share. . . . Being a dreamer by nature it's important to me to have someone who can believe as I do in distant goals and objectives, things not yet tried. In Carol Lynn I find this . . . Thank you for your wonderful daughter. I hope that I'll prove more worthy of her all the time."

"Gerald," I said one afternoon some weeks after our engagement. "What do you think about polygamy? Does it interest you?"

"Well, not at the moment."

"Ever?"

"What do I know about ever? No, I don't think so. Why?"

"I mean, does it sound good? Would you like to have more than one woman?"

Gerald shook his head seriously. "No."

"Well, that's a relief," I said.

Gerald laughed. I was used to people laughing when I brought up the subject, but to me, as a Mormon woman, it was serious business. Even though the Church had not practiced polygamy for a long time, there was still the threat. Ever since my religion teacher in high school had solemnly borne the class his testimony that polygamy was the divine order of marriage and would be restored again, certainty in the next world if not in this, there had been the threat. We would all be less selfish in the next world, he assured us, and we would not feel possessive about one another. If we lived worthily here, we would be candidates for the highest form of eternal progression. And one of the requirements would be to participate in God's true order of marriage, polygamy.

I sat riveted to my seat. I hated what I was hearing, but it was probably true. My religion teacher knew more about God's will than I did. I walked the six blocks to my house with an empty feeling in my stomach.

"Gerald, do you know that when I was in freshman English, Dr. Clark assigned us a theme on 'A Fate Worse Than Death.' Know what I wrote about?" I nodded my head. "Polygamy."

Gerald laughed again, a free, sympathetic laugh.

"He gave me an A but called me in to talk with him. He said, as everybody else had, that I really shouldn't worry about it, that if we get to the other side and find out that it *is* true, we'll be able to deal with it."

"I suppose we will," Gerald agreed.

"But, Gerald," I said urgently, "I don't *want* it to be okay. I *want* an exclusive relationship with someone, with you. I like the idea of two people being exclusively committed to each other. That's the only thing that makes sense to me."

Gerald listened carefully. Usually he was the one who went on and on about things he had strong feelings on, but now it was my turn.

"If we're going to live together, there is something you have to understand about me. I've got this . . . this *thing* about *women,* about how we look at women and how we're told they fit or don't fit into the scheme of things. Some things don't feel right to me. Some things seem terribly unjust. Some things seem . . . insane. Half the human family are women, but everything, practically *everything* is written out, is seen, is arranged from a male point of view. It's like maleness is first prize and femaleness is second prize all down the line. It's crazy!"

"I know what you mean, Blossom. I can see that." Good. Gerald wasn't laughing. He was taking this seriously. He wasn't like a lot of men who turned it all into a joke that ended in another female putdown. "Don't talk to me, talk to Eve. It's all her fault," a guy might say. Or, "Polygamy? Who'd want two women? One's enough to drive you crazy!" Gerald was not a macho male who had all the answers. We could explore and find out some things for ourselves.

Sometime in the first part of February, Gerald and I were walking from a movie on campus to my place, and he seemed worried. When I asked him what was wrong, Gerald sighed and put an arm around my shoulder. "Just life. I guess I want everything to be perfect, all the time. And when I see something not being perfect—like us not communicating as fully as I want us too—I get scared."

I stopped walking and looked up at him. "Gerald," I said, "your need for deep, intense communication sometimes scares me to death. I'm not used to that. I know that sometimes I'm flippant when you want to be serious, but I think we can handle it. If there's anything you want to talk about—*anything*—I'll try. Is there?"

Gerald hesitated. "Not now."

On Valentine's Day, after we had exchanged humorous cards and I had given Gerald a red-and-white cake, I went to get two plates and a knife.

"None for me right now, thanks," he said. "I'm fasting." And then he said, "Blossom, sit down."

I sat on the couch and Gerald pulled up the piano bench and sat directly facing me. Then he took my hands in his, bowed his head, and said a short prayer that we would be blessed in being able to communicate truly and to solve any difficulties we might have.

"Blossom," Gerald said, after a moment's silence, "there's something I have to tell you."

The pit of my stomach suddenly iced over and I felt myself shaking my head.

"I *need* to tell you," he went on. "I had thought maybe I didn't, but I do. Nothing stays new and perfect, I can see that." He was talking faster now. "And I think you can only solve problems if there's complete honesty."

He was quiet, staring at the rug as if his next lines might be written there.

"Gerald?" My mouth was dry. "Gerald? Has there been . . . a girl?"

Gerald looked up from the rug and into my eyes. "Not a girl. A guy. Guys, Blossom."

Guys? I sat stunned for a moment. Gerald had . . . ? Then a wave of relief flooded over me, taking with it the ice in my stomach. Guys. That wasn't as bad as if it had been girls. I had wanted to be Gerald's first real experience, and I still could be. That other—guys—that was not real. That was something strange that I did not understand, but it wasn't *real*. Of course, you're not supposed to do it. Gerald shouldn't have done it. But it can be repented of.

"Blossom, it will never happen again. I promise. That's not what I really am. I'm not really a"—it was hard for him to say the word—"a homosexual. That's all in the past now. What do you want to ask me? Ask anything you want."

I shook my head, opened my mouth, and then closed it again. "I don't understand. Why?"

Gerald spoke slowly, concerned about finding the right words. "In high school . . . it happened. . . . with a friend. It felt really wonderful—to have that kind of closeness. I know it was wrong, but somehow I *needed* it. I confessed to my bishop before I went on my mission. He wasn't sure I should go, so he sent me to a General Authority who is in charge of this problem, and they both—*both* of them felt that I had fully repented and that I should go. So I went. And I had a great mission. Nothing happened that way. But my friend from high school—he had wanted to go on a mission but decided he couldn't handle it—was having terrible problems. He was depressed and could hardly function. I tried to help him and . . . it happened again. I didn't mean it to."

I thought for a moment. "And Paul? What about Paul?"

Gerald nodded.

So. That had been why Paul was so cold to me. And why Gerald had moved out. They were lovers.

Gerald's grip on my hands tightened. "You can throw me out if you want to, Blossom." A smile began to form, loosening the tightness around his mouth. "But I sure do hope you won't because I love you. *This* is what I want, this that I have with you. And I want a family. I want children. We're going to be okay. I talked to my bishop again and he feels like I do, that if I have a woman that I really love, everything will be okay." Gerald paused, then continued in a very low and serious tone.

"I've had a very important, very personal experience—with Christ. To him, I'm okay. I know that. The problem is over, Blossom. If you still want me . . ."

I studied his face. It was the same face. Those were the same eyes. And in them was the same light, the same warmth, the same unmistakable goodness. I didn't search for what to say. I simply read what was written for me to say.

"Gerald." I took his face in my hands. "Of course I still want you. I'm not so concerned about what you've done as about what you *are*. I know what you are, I've seen deep inside of you, and I wouldn't give up all that beauty for anything. Of *course* I want you!"

"Oh, Blossom." Gerald kissed my hands. "You won't be sorry. I'm going to make you so happy. *So happy!*"

When Gerald left that night, I was not deeply troubled. I trusted him. I trusted my own feelings. And I trusted the position of the Church on the matter. All of us, I had been taught, were created heterosexual, and only the expression of that sexuality in marriage was acceptable before God. But some of us get off track. For some unknown reason, sometimes people of the same sex are attracted to one another that way, and if they act on it, it's a sin. So they repent. And they don't do it again. Those who don't repent get more and more involved until they're stuck being *real* homosexuals. Sinners.

Homosexuals. I had probably not said the word more than two or three times in my life. I grew up in Salt Lake City and then in Gusher on a farm without electricity or running water. My family background had given me little to go on about sex in its usual forms and certainly nothing about *unusual* sex. My parents once did give us a talk on why animals were doing what we sometimes saw them doing, but nothing was said about humans doing anything similar. If my three brothers, Donald, David, and Warren, or my sister, Marie, knew anything more about sex than I did, they didn't tell me.

Our move from Gusher to Provo when I was thirteen added to my education in some ways, but not regarding sex. Provo had been nicknamed Happy Valley. It was free from the disturbing influences that troubled the outside world, or so it seemed to me. We didn't know there was any such thing as homosexuals. We hardly knew there was any such thing as Democrats. We'd heard of blacks, but many of us had never seen one in person. I attended BYU high school, a laboratory school run by the university. As a takeoff on a television show of the day we nicknamed ourselves Purity Playhouse. Attending school at Purity Playhouse in the confines of Happy Valley made for a lot of insulation.

I tried to recall when I figured out what sex was all about. Probably when I started baby-sitting for some people who had a marriage manual on their bookshelf. That became my favorite place to baby-sit. When the kids were in bed I would carefully take the book from the shelf and—if there were potato chips in the cupboard and a handful wouldn't be missed—sit down to a sensual indulgence, eating potato chips and reading about this incredibly fascinating thing that men and women did together.

They did it after they were married, of course. And it was beautiful and rewarding and not only brought children but strengthened the bonds of the relationship. It sounded wonderful.

Whether or not I would follow the Church's moral code was never questioned, even when I was traveling and met all those strange and seductive Arabs and Italians and Israelis. Keeping myself clean for my temple marriage made perfect sense to me. I had known of a few girls who had to get married, and even one who lied to her bishop and went through her temple wedding ceremony two months pregnant. But as far as I knew, all of *my* friends were pure. And I came back from my year abroad having lost my luggage, but with my passport and virtue intact.

But boys were weaker. We had always been taught that.

23

Boys were more easily tempted, so it was up to girls to help them resist. Boys were told again and again not to touch girls. Was that maybe the reason why some boys touched each other? I didn't know. The whole idea was very strange. I had never had feelings like that. I had tremendous yearnings to be physically close to the couple of guys I had really liked, but never a girl. I tried now to imagine it. I almost laughed, and then felt a little sick. No, I would not like that. I would not like that at all. How could anybody? How could Gerald?

I must have been a senior in high school when I finally learned about homosexuals. One day on the stairs of the Arts Building, I saw some kids teasing and tickling a boy named Gene. Gene was the tallest person in the school, extremely thin, and he walked a little funny.

"You like boys, don't you, Gene?" said the guy who was holding Gene's arms back and laughing.

"Come on, admit it," said another one, tickling and punching lightly.

Gene was blushing and grinning in embarrassment, struggling to get free. "No. Hey, you guys. No."

"Gene likes boys!" said another, joining in.

A teacher came along and told them to clear the stairway. One of the girls I was with giggled, and when she told me what the boys meant, I was amazed. I probably said, "Gag a rag bag!"—our favorite expression for something gross.

I knew a few jokes about homosexuals, and when the Kinsey reports had come out, I read a little in the national magazines, feeling I had an obligation to learn what was happening in the outside world. I was sure my parents never knew even a tenth of this stuff. They couldn't have told us about it even if they'd wanted to, which of course they didn't. I had always assumed my parents had sex about five times, once for each of the five children: Well, four maybe, because of the twins.

But Kinsey gave a whole different view to the subject. He said that a large percentage of the male population experiments with some kind of homosexual behavior and that about 10 percent turn out to be basically homosexual. That sounded like a lot.

As far as I knew, Gerald was the only one I'd met who had even done any experimenting. And I was certain I didn't know any of the other kind—the *real* homosexuals—those who wouldn't repent and put their experiences behind them, as Gerald had.

How fortunate that Gerald and I had found each other. Marriage was the answer, the right, the wonderful answer to all this. No wonder marriage was a prerequisite to full salvation. And ours was going to be beautiful. Gerald enjoyed touching me. I knew that. And I loved touching him. It was indescribably delicious to me. Marriage was the answer.

Two weeks later, Gerald broke the engagement. I came home from work one day to find that he had cleared from my apartment the things he had been keeping there—his guitar, some record albums. I dialed his number, my hand shaking.

"Gerald? Don't you think we can handle whatever it is in a better way than this?"

"It's not going to work. It just won't work." And he hung up.

I was devastated. What had I done? Was this somehow my fault? I had known that Gerald was growing more discontent. He had suggested we memorize a scripture together every day and have daily prayer together to help us grow closer. I had been glad to do that.

Some of the early ecstasy had been dimming, but I had expected that. Nothing stays in its first stages. But it frightened Gerald. If it wasn't going to be perfect, he couldn't bear it. And maybe . . . was he embarrassed and ashamed at what he had told me about? Was he unsure of himself, that he could be a good husband?

"I'm not man enough for you," he said sadly when we finally talked the next week. "And you're not woman enough for me. It would be the blind leading the blind."

But five long months later he was back, more sure than ever that he loved me and needed me. "I was afraid," he said as we sat together on the bench that August evening in Pioneer Park. "I was a coward. But these last months have been hell for me. I know more than I ever knew before how much I need you. Can we try it again, Blossom?"

This time when I said yes, it was a wiser person who was speaking. No relationship is without its trials, and we had just gone through a major one, Gerald was sure now. He had spent five months agonizing over what it was he really wanted, who he really was, who I was, what we could or could not be together. Now he knew beyond any doubt that he wanted to marry me. Now he was sure.

Chapter 3

A Mormon temple wedding is the most beautiful ceremony I know. Ours was on September 9, 1966. Outside, on the face of the surrounding mountains, the business of change was visible, patches of red and gold burned between the green. And inside, within the gray granite walls of the Salt Lake Temple, the business of eternity was going on, the business of permanence, of commitment, of forever.

There we were in a small "sealing room," Gerald and I, dressed in white, facing each other across a velvet altar, surrounded by our family and friends. Little bursts of light came from the hundred chandeliers in the mirrors that were set to catch eternity.

Elder Hanks, in a white suit, was speaking to us on the importance of marriage. His face was radiant. "I remember the story of the pioneer sister who wrote in her diary one night while crossing the plains, 'Today I lost my best friend.' She was speaking of her husband. That's what I hope for you, Gerald and Carol Lynn. Be one another's best friend. Every couple will have differences. We can approach them in two ways: to win a contest or to solve a problem. Whatever problems you meet, let love come first."

Gerald and I then joined hands across the altar and were "sealed" together as husband and wife in the presence of

"God, angels, and these witnesses." Sealed for "time and all eternity."

My father shook hands with Gerald, and his voice quavered a little as he said, "Young man, you be good to this girl. I charge you with the responsibility of making her happy. She's very special to me."

"To me too, sir," Gerald replied. "Believe me, her happiness is as important to me as my own."

"It was a lovely wedding, Sis," Daddy said, hugging me. "I think your mother was here. I just spoke to Aunt Cree, and she said she was as sure as anything that your mother was here."

We drove to our four-day honeymoon in the little blue Volkswagen we had bought the month before. Gerald opened the sunroof and the early afternoon light poured in. I had not wanted to spend the extra two hundred dollars for the sunroof, but Gerald had been so charmingly insistent that I had given in. Gerald was not a minimalist. I had already learned that. He *needed* a sunroof. And I needed him to be happy.

On our way up to the cabin we stopped at Heber to buy groceries. "Oh, hey," said Gerald as we pushed the cart down the canned food aisle. "Oysters! I hear they're a great aphrodisiac. Let's get some."

I laughed. "Well, I won't be needing oysters. Will you?"

"No, I don't think so, but"—he tossed a couple of cans into the cart—"better safe than sorry."

I turned away and giggled as the clerk rang up the oysters.

As we went up into the canyon we were surrounded by the magic of the season, the changing leaves of the aspens, and the steady color of the evergreens. After we carried our bags and the groceries into the cabin, we stretched out on the bed. We hugged and kissed a minute, and then I pulled away and sat up.

"Gerald, I . . . before we go any further, there's something I have to tell you."

Gerald looked at me seriously. "Yes?"

"This is not easy, Gerald," I said, and took a deep breath, "but there's something about me you don't know. I've been putting off telling you, but it can't wait any longer."

Gerald cautiously leaned up on one elbow and studied my face.

"What?"

Slowly I raised my hand to my head, and then quickly pulled off the little wiglet that had served to add body to the top of my short hairdo.

Gerald collapsed into laughter. He rolled and doubled up and rolled again. He laughed until he cried. Then he pulled me down beside him and kissed me.

"How long have you been planning that?" he asked.

"Since the first moment I saw you."

"Is that *all*?" he asked. "Does anything else come off?"

"Nope. That's it. Everything else is real. Some things are not much—as you will soon see—but real."

He laughed again and wiped his eyes on the pillowcase. "Oh, Blossom. Life with you is going to be something!"

That night the warmth of the fire, the soft glow of the kerosene lanterns, the sound of crickets and frogs and coyotes, all provided a stage for the wonderful action of love. We did not need the oysters. I have only the best memories of my wedding night. And of the nights and the days that followed. I thought that if Gerald had had any apprehensions about whether or not he would be able to perform well with a woman, they should now be put to rest.

Gerald was a good husband. He was industrious and creative and reliable. He made and decorated our wedding cake for the reception that was held that weekend. He set out with great energy to make our apartment a charming place, painting, paneling, and arranging. He had Mario paint a mural of blossoms on the kitchen wall. All we could afford to buy was a blue rug and a hanging lamp and a bed, so Gerald decided to build a couch. We went up the canyon and brought back slabs of gray shale that he used to face a frame he built. Topped with cushions of blue and wine corduroy, it was a stunning piece of furniture.

I continued to work as a scriptwriter for BYU motion pictures, and Gerald continued to go to school full-time, to act in plays, and work part-time in the bakery. He was determined not to let me be the sole financial support of the family, but on the day that he dozed off in a large vat of frosting, with the pink sticky stuff up to his armpit, we decided he should quit his job and just concentrate on school.

I was happy and I knew that Gerald was happy. We laughed a lot, talked a lot, and were tender a lot. We played endless games of Scrabble and Authors, and laughed because we could never remember which Mark Twain card was missing—was it Huckleberry Finn or Tom Sawyer? There were serious things going on in the outside world. The nation was divided over support for the war in Vietnam, there was war in the Middle East, and there were race riots in Detroit. But Gerald and I were happily ensconced in Provo, Utah, in our little apartment with the blue rug and the rock couch and each other.

Times of tension and minor resentments were generally handled with humor. For example, it was Gerald's job every Wednesday evening to take the garbage can out to the curb. Since he often forgot, I had taken to reminding him, which, he said, made him feel like a little boy. For three weeks in December I watched the garbage pile up until I decided to write a letter: "Dear Mr. Pearson, All your friends here at the Department of Public Utilities have been saying to one another, 'Whatever happened to the Pearsons' garbage? They used to be among our best customers, but for the last three weeks they have not left for us so much as a banana peel.' Won't you please join the millions who know the joy of giving this season and remember your friends at the garbage collection department? Wishing you a happy, garbage-free new year . . ." I made the envelope look as official as possible and mailed it.

The next day when I came home from work Gerald was going through the mail. I went in the other room to change clothes. There was Gerald's laugh. "Blossom! Come *here!*"

I stood in the doorway buttoning a shirt as he said, "You will never *believe* this letter we just got from the garbage men. Listen!"

He read the first line and then glanced up to see me holding my mouth and sliding down the woodwork. Gerald put the letter down.

"*You* did it!" he said. He picked up the envelope and looked at it. "*You did it!*" Then he laughed and lunged at me and tickled me until I could not breathe.

Gerald and I did have different philosophies on some things. He always did everything in a big way. He could not do something small. When Mario and Dana ran out of food, Gerald delivered to their house one hundred pounds of potatoes. I laughed that day, but some days I did not laugh. Gerald was a spender and I was a saver, both financially and emotionally. Gerald had an appetite for emotional exchange and deep, soulful sharing that was voracious. Sometimes I felt like an audience during his hours of philosophizing and probing. It was as if he had complex and pressing hungers that I could not even name. His appetite for knowing and experiencing sometimes frightened me.

That was what prompted my dream, I suppose. It was the only dream I had ever had from which I woke up sobbing. Gerald had gotten up early to study for a test and I was still asleep. From the front room he heard me crying and rushed in to see what was the matter. He had to shake me to wake me up.

"What is it, Blossom? What's wrong?"

I was tremendously relieved to come back to reality. "Oh, I was dreaming. It's so *silly*. Why am I crying?"

In the dream, Gerald and I were in a bakery. On all sides were shelves of cookies. Signs were posted saying, cookies— one dollar each. Gerald went wild. He was going from stack to stack grabbing as many cookies as his arms could hold. "No, Gerald, no," I cried out to him. "Don't. It's not worth it. A dollar a cookie is not worth it. Please don't!" But Gerald wasn't listening. He could not grab the cookies fast enough. I was filled with terror. "Don't, Gerald!" I screamed. "It's not worth it!" And then I woke up crying.

Gerald put his arms around me and wiped my face. "Don't worry, Blossom; I promise, I *promise* that I will never buy cookies for a dollar each. Okay?"

About eight months after we were married Gerald called me, excited, at work.

"Blossom, there's a letter here from the Utah State Office of Fine Arts. Can I open it?"

"Quick!" I had submitted a comedy to the playwriting division and had been anxiously awaiting news.

"'Dear Mrs. Pearson,'" Gerald read. "'We are happy to inform you that you are the first-place winner.' Oh, wow, Blossom! First place! Congratulations!"

I shrieked. "What else? What else?"

Gerald's voice exploded with excitement. "A thousand dollars. Blossom, you get *a thousand dollars*!"

We celebrated that night. With food, of course. Gerald went to the store and splurged, and we invited Mario and Dana to come to our feast.

"To Blossom," said Mario, raising his glass of ice water. "May she get famouser and famouser and richer and richer."

"Oh, she will, she will," said Gerald earnestly. "I'm going to see to that. For the *first* thing, we're going to get those poems of hers published."

"Oh, Gerald," I sighed. We had been over this before. I enjoyed writing, and some of my poems had been published in Church magazines, but to try to publish a *book* seemed terribly immodest. "I *told* you I want to do that posthumously."

"Not good enough," said Gerald. "People need these. Now."

Mario and Dana joined Gerald and ganged up on me. Dana had used a number of my poems in a lesson she had given to the Relief Society women in her ward and had found many of them moved to tears. (A ward is a Mormon geographical division, and the Relief Society is the women's organization.) By the time the evening was done we had laid a plan. That weekend the four of us would go up in the mountains and organize the poems into a book. Reluctantly I agreed.

It was windy on the mountain and we had to put rocks on the piles of poems to keep them from blowing away. There was a pile for the yes's, for the no's, and for the maybe's.

"Now here's a yes, a definite yes," said Mario. "Listen. 'Of Places Far.'"

> To me Istanbul
> Was only a name,
> Until a picture
> You took
> Of the Blue Mosque
> Came.

I don't receive
Postcards from heaven
Showing Saint Peter
At prayer,
But, oh—that place
Is real enough,
Now that
You are there.

I kept my eyes on the ground; it always embarrassed me to listen to something I'd written. I'd written that for me and my mother and nobody else had any business looking at it. This was not such a good idea.

"And definitely this one," said Gerald enthusiastically.

I couldn't stare at the ground while Gerald read. I stared at his face. He was having a marvelous time mapping out his crazy plans for my poems. He was loving this. "Beginnings," Gerald read.

Today
You came running
With a small specked egg
Warm in your hand.
You could barely understand,
I know,
As I told you
Of beginnings—
Of egg and bird.
Told, too,
That years ago
You began,
Smaller than sight.
And then,
As egg yearns for sky
And seed
Stretches to tree,

34

You became,
Like me.

Oh,
But there's so much more.
You and I, child,
Have just begun.
Think:
Worlds from now
What might we be?—
We,
Who are seed
Of Deity.

Thoughtfully Gerald put the poem under the yes rock. "That's not a bad title for the book," he said. *"Beginnings. Let's call it Beginnings."*

Soon Gerald had some fine illustrations drawn by our good friend Trevor Southey, and he put me, the drawings, and the manuscript in the car and drove up to Salt Lake City to see who would be first in line to publish the book.

"Poetry?" said the first and only publisher we talked to. "Nobody buys poetry. I couldn't possibly publish a book of poetry."

"Could I just read—" I began.

"Save your breath. If Shakespeare walked in here I wouldn't publish his poetry."

"We have some great illustrations," said Gerald, holding up a lovely drawing called *God in Embryo.*

"Hmm. Looks pretty depressing to me. Sorry. Poetry won't sell. Thanks for thinking of us."

On the way home I told Gerald it was back to my original suggestion—publishing the book posthumously.

"Nope," he said. "It's going to be published now."

"By whom?"

"By me. I'm going to become a publisher. I'll go to the

credit union and borrow the money, and then just do it."

I had learned by now that it was a losing battle to try to dissuade Gerald from something he had really decided to do.

Two months later two thousand copies of a slim white volume called *Beginnings* were ready at the bindery. Gerald and Mario borrowed a truck and went to pick them up. I was terrified. We put them in the closet and under the bed and in my father's garage.

"Well," I said, that first night as we sat staring at the stacks of packages, "at least we've got our two year's supply of wedding presents."

"Wedding presents, nothing," said Gerald. "These books are going to sell. Know what the manager of the bindery told, me this afternoon? 'I sure am glad to see this book get out of here.' 'What do you mean?' I asked him. He smiled and said, 'Well, I went back there yesterday to see how work was going and everything had ground to a halt. All the help were sitting around reading poems to each other!'" Gerald threw back his head and laughed. "Fasten your seat belt, Blossom!"

The next morning we took some books up to the bookstore on the BYU campus. "Poetry?" said the buyer. "Nobody buys poetry."

"Could you just put up a display?" asked Gerald. "You know, LOCAL POET WRITES BOOK."

"Well," she hesitated. "I'll take four, on consignment."

We persuaded her to take a package of twenty on consignment and went home.

Later that afternoon Gerald hung up the telephone and screamed. "Blossom! They sold them all! They want some more!" He danced me around the kitchen, then grabbed three more packages and raced out to the car.

In the first week the BYU bookstore had sold 200 copies and within two months they had sold 1,600 copies. A similar thing was happening in other Utah bookstores. Early on, we had to order 5,000 copies more to prepare for the Christmas sales.

"Sister Pearson?" I became used to answering the phone and hearing the request. "The women in our ward are so thrilled with your poems. Could you come and speak to us next month?" I found myself going out frequently, always amazed that I seemed able to move and to lift people.

Letters began to arrive, telling me how my writing had affected people. "For several months I was in a suicidal depression. Without your poems I really don't know if I would be here today." "Thanks so much for being our voice. I find that I can't give a talk or a lesson now without using at least one of your poems." "Your book has aroused such a well of emotion in me that I must write and tell you I feel my life richer and my love of God deeper because of you."

The spring after *Beginnings* came out, I was invited to give a program to the wives of the General Authorities of the Church at their monthly luncheon in the Lion House in Salt Lake City. It was like a command performance for royalty, and I was so nervous as I climbed the stairs that when I reached the landing and was greeted by the hostess, I stammered, "I—I'm Carol Lynn Poetry and I'm here to read p—" (Gerald couldn't stop laughing when I told him that one and it became one of his favorite stories.)

By the time it was my turn to perform, however, I had recovered my wits. As I began my introduction, Jesse Evans Smith, the wife of our prophet in those, days, sang out uninhibitedly, "Dear! I hope you're going to read the poem on page forty-two. That's my favorite one!" I assured her that I would, and when I read the poem she beamed, mouthing every memorized word along with me.

I watched Gerald humming as he opened the orders and packed the books and organized the bookkeeping. He was so happy. So proud of me, so unabashedly delighted that his wife was becoming a local celebrity. *How many men would do that*, I wondered. *Who else would borrow money to publish his wife's poems? Nobody in his right mind.* But I was glad Gerald was not in his right mind. He had soared into my life like a wild, bright comet and was rearranging my entire solar system. He was taking all my dreams and making them realities.

As we concluded our first year of marriage, I was immensely satisfied. I had been right. Marriage was the answer, for both of us. The rightness of it was symbolized in the male and female bronze figures in the sculpture Trevor had made and called "Resurrection." Gerald had purchased the male figure, which had been completed first, and then for our wedding anniversary he had given me the female figure. The solitary male figure had looked so incomplete, lonely as the first moments of Eden before whatever was, was mystically divided and became two. Adam and Eve. Gerald and Blossom.

On a Sunday morning we were lazing in bed waiting for the time to get ready for Church. Gerald seemed in a pensive mood and didn't want to talk. He turned on the radio to listen, as he often did, to the Sunday morning poetry reading on KSL. The rich male voice introduced the next poem, "The Buried Life," by Matthew Arnold. I watched Gerald's face as he listened, absorbed.

> . . . Alas! is even love too weak
> to unlock the heart, and let it speak?
> Are even lovers powerless to reveal
> To one another what indeed they feel?
> I knew the mass of men concealed
> Their thoughts, for fear that if revealed
> They would by other men be met
> With blank indifference, or with blame
>   reproved;
> I knew they lived and moved
> Tricked in disguises, alien to the rest
> Of men, and alien to themselves—and yet
> The same heart beats in every human breast!

There were tears on Gerald's cheeks. *Why were there tears on Gerald's cheeks?* He took a long, loud breath and stared at the ceiling.

> But often, in the world's most crowded streets,
> But often, in the din of strife,
> There rises an unspeakable desire
> After the knowledge of our buried life;
> A thirst to spend our fire and restless force
> In tracking out our true, original course;
> A longing to inquire
> Into the mystery of this heart which beats
> So wild, so deep in us—to know
> Whence our lives come and where they go.

Gerald cried quietly, and then gave himself over to great heaving sobs. I was paralyzed. What was this? Gerald was my rock. I couldn't have him shaking like this. I pulled him into my arms and pressed my cheek to his hair. He let me comfort him for a moment, and then turned away.

"It's nothing," he said in a strange voice. "It's just . . . me. Just life."

I took his hand and was quiet. *No one can be strong all the time*, I thought. Anything so bright as he would have to have a dark side. I'll just let it be and it will take care of itself. Gerald can handle anything. He'll be fine. We'll be fine. In a few minutes he'll turn over and look at me and smile. And then we'll get up and go to Church.

Chapter 4

When I went in November to my first appointment with Dr. Webster, Gerald said, "You just *better* be pregnant, Blossom. And if you're not, don't come home until you are!"

I was. We were both thrilled. Despite all my questions on the role and the status of women, I felt that nothing in life would be more significant than giving life. By myself I would be terrified of facing something so huge. But Gerald had a talent for making things work. Gerald fed me soda crackers and took over even more of the household responsibilities and put his ear to my abdomen daily to keep up on developments. I arranged to work free-lance for the film studio and set up my typewriter on the kitchen table.

One afternoon Gerald came bounding in from his day on campus. "Blossom! Guess what? They're taking a play to Europe for three months and Dr. Hansen wants me to go!"

"Europe?"

Gerald straddled a chair and drew it up so his face was close to mine. "I told him I didn't think I could go."

I burst out laughing. What he was really saying was, "Can I go? Huh? Can I go?"

I reached over and gave him a resounding kiss, and then said, "Of course you can go, Gerald. Of *course* you can!"

"Really? But, Blossom, this is *now*. I mean, while you're still pregnant. I can't go off and leave you pregnant! And we . . . I mean *they* won't be back until the first part of June. That's just a couple of weeks before the baby's due. What if he comes early? I don't think I should go."

I quickly filled the scales and watched the balance. On the one hand I didn't want Gerald to go. I would miss him. I had never been pregnant before and didn't want to go through this time alone. And maybe the baby *would* come early, though most first babies don't. But on the other hand—oh, on the other hand, Europe! For Gerald to be able to spend three months in Europe would be a priceless experience. Nobody deserved such an experience more than he did. He would drink it all in like a thirsty man, getting every drop of learning and pleasure. I had regretted that sometimes my experiences outweighed Gerald's. I wanted him to see Michelangelo's *David* and Tivoli Gardens and the *Mona Lisa*. And to have the experience of touring, of setting up and taking down and performing and learning more about the theater. Thud. The scale was set. Hadn't he given his all to helping my work? I wanted to give Gerald the world; the least I could do was to give him Europe. I would be brave like the pioneer women who sent their men away on missions and endured the hardships with good cheer.

"Of course you can go!" I said.

I watched the airplane move down the runway and take off. I had told each of the fifteen members of the touring group to take good care of Gerald. They were good people, all of them. I was glad Gerald would be with such good people.

He wrote me loving and descriptive letters. The troops were enjoying *Bye Bye Birdie*. It was just the kind of frivolous entertainment needed to buoy up the servicemen. The group was having a good time, and Gerald was stunned with all the wonderful things he was seeing. And he still loved me.

"Dearest Blossom," he wrote. "Of all the things I've seen in the whole world, you're still my favorite. I love you so very, very much! You've such a wonderful place in my heart clear over here. I can feel a oneness with you that I never want to lose. I think of you constantly and when I'm not thinking of you, I'm talking of you. Tomorrow I'm going to pack you in my little shoulder bag that I bought and take you exploring Heidelberg with me. It should be great fun."

And I, at home, waited for his letters and slept on his side of the bed to feel closer to him. I wrote Gerald of the continuing sale of our book, and of a play he wrote being chosen for production as a finalist in the State Fine Arts Competition, and of my delight in finding each week a gift he had hidden somewhere in the house and devised clues for (under the piano lid was a tiny pair of red booties). And I wrote him my love. "I miss the bells on our door clanging as you come in. And I miss holding hands with you in Church. And I miss hugging you in the middle of the night. And I miss praying with you. And I miss the good things that you help me to be."

I wrote a lullaby for our baby and sang it with my guitar onto a tape. Gerald wrote that he played it over and over again.

Gerald's letters began to tell of some struggles he was experiencing and then had resolved. In his last letter he wrote, "I have such hopes for the joy that I want to bring into your life. I am coming home to you a much stronger person, a much better husband. I hope that I can sustain the growth that I've found here."

On June 12, 1968, Gerald ran the length of the corridor of the Salt Lake airport to greet me, a Scottish tam on his head, a Scottish scarf streaming behind him, and tears coursing down his face.

"Blossom! Blossom!"

I ran to meet him, as fleetly as one can who is nine months pregnant. Life had continued while Gerald was gone, but how good it was to have him back with me, where he belonged.

In the car driving home, I noticed that Gerald was wearing a new ring, a green stone in a gold setting. He wore it just above his wedding ring.

"Jess gave it to me," he explained. "A friendship ring. He's a great guy and he's helped me a lot to understand some things. I'll tell you all about it sometime."

Nine days after Gerald's arrival I woke up at three in the morning with contractions. If it wasn't the real thing, I didn't want to bother Gerald. The doctor said I should head for the hospital when they were three minutes apart. Were they? I did not want to turn on the light to check the clock. A sonnet, I knew, took exactly one minute to recite aloud. "How do I love thee?" I mouthed. "Let me count the ways." Three times through. " . . . I shall but love thee better after death." There was another contraction. Life was at the door.

"Gerald." I turned on the light. "Gerald, wake up. We're going to have a baby!"

I have never known a man more anxious to be a father, or to be a good father. I was not having the baby, *we* were having the baby. Before we went to the hospital Gerald laid his hands on my head and gave me a blessing that all would go well. In the labor room he held my legs when they shook from the pain and told me I was doing fine and that it would soon be done. And when I was wheeled from the delivery room, under the comforting warmth of a blanket, with Emily on my breast, Gerald was ecstatic.

"Oh, Blossom, you did it! You did it! She's beautiful. Did you know I love you, Blossom?"

Nursing was the only thing that Gerald reluctantly did not share. He changed the baby, bathed her, handed her to me in the middle of the night, and held her for long hours.

"Did you know," he said to me one evening as he rocked Emily in the wooden rocker that had belonged to my mother. "Did you know that babies can die if they're not touched? That book I'm reading—*Touching* by Ashley Montague—says that in orphanages where babies are fed and cleaned but never held, a lot of them just die, turn their face to the wall and die. And when nurses are hired to come in and touch and hold them, the babies stop dying. Isn't that amazing, Blossom?"

I sometimes felt that heaven misfired and shot Gerald by mistake into the twentieth century when he should have appeared in a white toga on the landscape of ancient Athens bouncing the meaning of life back and forth with Socrates. He never stopped reading, and he never stopped talking. Sometimes I would go to sleep in the middle of a lengthy passage that inspired him from William James, Wilhelm Reich, Evelyn Underhill, or Abraham Maslow. It was as if he felt an urgent need to convince me of something, but I was never quite sure what it was.

I was stirring something at the stove one evening, half listening to Gerald talk. "And so, maybe there *is* some kind of validity to other arrangements—like polygamy."

"What?"

"I said that maybe there is some validity to other ways of looking at relationships besides our traditional one-man-one-woman exclusive arrangement."

Why was that strange chill traveling through me? Gerald was just philosophizing. It didn't mean a thing.

"Are you trying to tell me you want to take another wife, Gerald?" I joked. "Be sure to tell me first so I can move out."

"Now, Blossom, don't get testy. Are you even listening to me? Sometimes I think you aren't even listening to me. This is important."

"Why so important? It's all theoretical. It doesn't really mean a thing."

"It means something to *me*." Gerald spoke faster. "Love—physical love—sex—is an exchange of energy that endows both people with *more* energy. And maybe for people to put such strict limits on it is not necessarily best. We can love more than one person. Maybe the final ideal is that I should be able to love everyone just as much as I love you." He looked at me almost as if he had made a request.

"But not in the same *way*, Gerald. Certainly we love everyone, but we don't *make love* to everyone!"

Gerald was trying to be patient and controlled. "All I'm saying, Blossom, is that if there are people who see physical love differently than you do, that maybe you should try to understand it. Like polygamy . . ."

"Why should I? In the first place, what you're talking about does not feel even remotely right. And in the second place, it has nothing to do with me."

"Well, maybe," Gerald spoke seriously, "maybe it does."

I pushed the pan to the back of the stove so it wouldn't burn and ran into the bedroom crying. I shut the door and threw myself onto the bed. Why was Gerald talking like this? And why was I letting it bother me? It was stupid. We were never going to have to deal with polygamy or . . . or anything. But what was that cold feeling in my stomach?

The following spring when Gerald graduated we went to spend the summer in Scotland and London. *Beginnings* had earned enough money for us to treat ourselves. We settled for seven weeks on Tiree, an island in the Hebrides off the Scottish coast. Our life there was peaceful and simple. We relied on each other, taking turns getting up with Emily, who said her first word and took her first step. We each had five or more good hours in the day for writing or study. Just before supper we would walk to the butcher to select a fine piece of meat for a very low price.

I wrote a play, a musical based on a Mormon pioneer experiment in communal living, *The Order Is Love.* My life was charmed and blessed. Even in the middle of the night it never got totally dark on Tiree. I went walking once at three in the morning and I could see the trees and the sheep. *Is this what heaven will be like?* I wondered. All light and no darkness.

Light was what intrigued Gerald. He was formulating a theory that all life is light, which is love. He had already gone through the New Testament, exclaiming anew over such scriptures as "I am the light of the world," and "God is love." And now he was doing the same thing with a Mormon scripture, the Doctrine and Covenants. "Listen to this, Blossom! Just listen to this," he would say to me several times a day, as if he had just received a personal revelation.

Gerald was determined to *know,* to break through what seemed and find out what really was. It was as if he had more puzzles in front of him than most people. Ordinary folk are content to just keep breathing in and out and let life flow around them. Gerald had to stop life at every turn and shake it by the shoulders and say, "What do you *mean?*"

After Tiree we went to London for five weeks of play going and sightseeing. As Gerald scanned the newspaper with pen in hand, making a list of the plays we wanted to see, he wrote down another title. "And definitely this one," he said, "*The Boys in the Band.* I really want to see it. And I want you to see it."

"What's it about?"

"Homosexuals."

"Oh. Okay, I guess I can handle that." I was surprised that there would be an actual play on the stage about homosexuals. Wasn't that pretty daring?

The play was gripping. So that's what homosexuals looked like, talked like. Eight men at a birthday party. I watched as I would watch at the scene of an accident. I almost wanted to cover my eyes and yet I couldn't look away. They were so pitiful! They were so intensely determined to be happy, to make it be all right. Their laughter was so brittle, so cold. Suddenly Alan joined the party, a "straight" friend of Michael's from college, whom we soon learn is a latent homosexual himself, alone in New York, having just left his wife and two children. Oh, Alan, I begged as I watched, don't do it. You don't want this. Look how empty it is. Look how tortured Hank is because his lover, Larry, cannot possibly be faithful to him. Look how driven Donald is with his Valium and his unending analysis. Look how pitiful Cowboy is, the beautiful boy purchased for the night as a present. Look how miserable Emory is behind his desperate humor. Look what a sorry lot they all are as they let down their façades. Oh, Alan, don't.

Alan heard me. At the end of the play he called his wife and told her he loved her and was sorry and would be back on the next plane. Probably everyone around me heard me sigh in relief. Oh, Alan, you have done the right thing. Like Gerald you have done the right thing. You won't be sorry.

I reached over and took Gerald's hand. How grateful he must be that I saved him from all of that. I wouldn't suggest it, of course. And I wouldn't bring up his past. I hadn't brought it up once in all the time we had been married. We would talk about the play in general, but we wouldn't make it personal. Still, how grateful Gerald must be.

Back in Utah we bought a large brick home and settled into family living. Our house was right across the street from a baseball park, and every evening in the summer the sounds of the game floated through our open windows. One evening I happened to come into the front room just as a huge burst of applause erupted from the fans across the street. I bowed and said, "Well, thank you. Thank you very much."

Gerald laughed and grabbed me and hugged me. "Oh, Blossom, how did I get you?"

I loved to make Gerald laugh. Seeing him happy was the great joy of my life. And to know that we were just beginning was a great wonder. We would be laughing and loving forever and ever.

Two additional children, John and Aaron, soon came. Gerald was allowed into the delivery room for these births and stood by my head in his white paper gown and cap like a good angel.

I loved being a mother, and I was very conscientious, making sure the children ate well and didn't watch very much television and learned to read early and were polite. The children knew that I loved them. But Gerald was a better playmate than I. There was more of the child left in him than in me.

It was Gerald who inaugurated "hugging time." In the mornings after he and I had hugged for a minute or two, we called out together, "Hugging time! Hugging time!" And three little streaks of light would burst into the room and onto the bed for five or ten minutes of hugging and laughing.

And it was Gerald who started the children on piano lessons as soon as their fingers could manage. And who would ask Emily about the history of the theater from Aristophanes to Shakespeare when she could barely talk: "And Emily, name three famous American playwrights."

"Three famous American playwrights," Emily would say, "are Arthur Miller, who wrote *Death of a Salesman,* Tennessee Williams, who wrote *The Glass Menagerie,* and Carol Lynn Pearson, who wrote *Pegora the Witch.*"

And it was Gerald who took all three camping for a week while I wrote day and night and finished a play before they got home, a piece that poured from my struggles with the woman question, *I Was a P.O.W. in the Battle of the Sexes.*

Friends of mine were envious that I had a husband who was so involved with the children. And who did a lot of the cooking. And who helped around the house. And who sympathized with my questions about the place of woman. And who encouraged me to accept the invitation to serve on Utah's Bicentennial Commission. And who held things together while I traveled on speaking engagements as far as Florida and Canada.

But Gerald was also busy with plenty of his own work. He became involved as a volunteer with The Group, a drug rehabilitation group composed of young Mormon flower children who had been through the drug-culture adventures of the sixties and were trying to straighten themselves out. Gerald seemed to know how to talk to the young man who had miraculously been off heroin for months now, to the fifteen-year-old redhead who had refused to get out of bed for weeks because the voices in his mind told him he was dead, and to the sweet-faced, long-haired girl who wandered in her mind and wandered on the streets. From his experiences with the group, he wrote and published a book, *There Is a Way Back*, that was directed to those who were still struggling.

"Regardless of what others may think of you," Gerald wrote, "or what they may have said about you, regardless of what you may be thinking of yourself, in the eyes of your Father in Heaven you are still holy ground."

"Well, Blossom, it's happened," said Gerald one evening. "I'm going to prison."

"For life?" I didn't look up from the book I was reading.

"For Mutual. It's a new Church calling. I get to work with the men in minimum security. Isn't that *great*?"

Another group of people for Gerald to feed. And he fed them, preparing inspiring lessons and spending more time than was required, encouraging the men who wanted to stay after and talk.

And there was enough left over for anybody else that Gerald saw in need. There was Blake, a newly returned missionary who lived just across the park and had been suddenly struck with encephalitis. The whole ward prayed for him during the several months he was in the hospital in a coma.

When he regained consciousness he had lost many of his physical capacities and came home to start the long road to partial recovery. Night after night Gerald walked across the park to read to him.

I was grateful that Gerald had so much to give, and only occasionally did his generous spirit trouble me; only occasionally did the storms that sometimes heaved within him cause me concern. Now and then I glimpsed something behind the light in his eyes that I did not understand. One night before going to sleep he read aloud passionately a poem by Walt Whitman.

Halfway through I felt that strange chill in my stomach. Why was his voice so excited?

> O to speed where there is space enough
>   and air enough at last!
> To be absolv'd from previous ties and
>   conventions. . . .
> To escape utterly from others' anchors
>   and holds!
> To drive free! To love free!
> To dash reckless and dangerous!
> To court destruction with taunts, with
>   invitations!
> To ascend, to leap to the heavens of the
>   love indicated to me!
> To rise thither with my inebriate soul!
> To be lost if it must be so!
> To feed the remainder of life with one hour
>   of fulness and freedom!
> With one brief hour of madness and joy.

"Isn't that incredible?" Gerald leaned back and closed his eyes.

"There are some vivid images there," I said.

"Blossom!" Gerald exploded and the muscles of his face tightened as they always did when he was exasperated with me. "You are so cerebral! So *cerebral*! Don't you feel things? Can't you feel what Whitman is doing in this poem?"

"Well, he's a little crazy, isn't he? To court destruction with invitations?"

"To risk, Blossom. To risk!" Gerald's voice was patient and slow, "To try for the very most, not to settle for the least. To really know, really experience, really live. To sell everything for the pearl of great price, whatever it may be!"

I looked down and picked at the bedspread. At times like this I was so intimidated by Gerald's force that I could not frame an intelligent sentence in response. And he would look at me pleading and disappointed. "Gerald, I'm sorry. It's just that I get uncomfortable when I see you so restless and questioning."

"Don't you question things, Blossom? Isn't there anything that you really question? That drives you?"

That was easy. "Of course. You know that, Gerald. I question our view of women. I question why femaleness seems not as valid as maleness is. *That* drives me. I would risk a lot to understand that, to do something about that."

Gerald nodded. He liked to have me speak strongly. And he understood and agreed with everything I had said on the matter.

"I know, Blossom. I know you feel strongly about that. So please, please try to understand some of the things that are important to me."

We kneeled for our usual evening prayer, and then pulled up the covers.

"Blossom?"

"What?"

"Did you know that Walt Whitman was a homosexual?"

I paused for a moment. "No. No, I did not."

Chapter 5

When Bobbie called me on the phone that September morning in 1974, I was just going up to my room over the garage to do my three hours of writing. Lynn Ann, a college student, would come in during that time to take over the household while I worked.

"Carol Lynn? This is Bobbie. Can I come over and talk to you?" She sounded troubled.

"Bobbie, are you okay?"

"Yeah, yeah," she said quickly. "It's . . . uh . . . not about me. It's about . . . Gerald."

"Oh? Well, listen, Bobbie. I'm just in the middle of preparing a talk I've got to give at BYU tomorrow. This morning's my only chance. How about tonight?"

"Okay."

"Let me get the kids into bed. How about nine o'clock?"

"Okay."

What in the world was Bobbie up to no? I wondered as I hung up the telephone. I had met her a few months before, when she drove up to our home on her motorcycle, wearing a black leather jacket and a helmet over her short, brown hair. I invited her in. I was used to unusual people coming in and out, especially since my second book of poetry had been published.

"Sister Pearson?" The "sister" took me aback. The Mormon form of address and the tough look seemed strangely mated.

"Yes?" She pulled out some papers from her pocket. "Well, I've got some poems I wrote here, and I wondered if you'd take a look at them and tell me if they're any good."

We talked for a couple of hours and I found out that Bobbie was nineteen and came from a Mormon family, but had dropped out a few years before. She had drifted around and had given birth to a child whom she had placed for adoption. She said she didn't like the life she was leading and wanted to get back in the Church.

I insisted she come with me—black leather jacket and all—to a poetry reading I was doing that evening. Afterward she seemed inspired to straighten out her life. We arranged that I would call her every Sunday morning so that she could tell me how she was doing. I checked on her regularly and she came over from time to time, reporting uneven progress but always determination. By September she had dropped the "Sister Pearson" and I was Carol Lynn.

Something about Gerald?

Gerald had left the day before to attend a workshop in California given by Robert Monroe, who had written a book on out-of-the-body experiences. He had continued his intense study of psychic and spiritual phenomena, and I was distressed, as were a few of our friends, that his search brought a certain alienation from the Church. I had read enough that I could not easily discount the whole thing and I prayed he would find what he was looking for. "Going within" had become a watchword for Gerald. He was even teaching classes in the basement on meditation, and he had bought a small system designed for Kirlian photography, to take pictures of the human aura, the "astral" or "spirit" body. He had high hopes for the workshop. Could he, like many he had read about, use meditation and focus to *will* higher states of consciousness, even out-of-the-body experiences?

Probably that's what was troubling Bobbie. She was trying very hard to be orthodox and must be worried about Gerald's odd studies. I'd have to tell her not to be too concerned. Gerald could handle it.

In my office, I pulled out the files I wanted and sat down at my desk. The talk was pretty well framed in my mind. "The World of Women." What a dumb title. But that was the theme of the faculty wives' luncheon tomorrow, so I would use it. My own womanly world was fine. I loved being the mother of three children. Plus I had a successful career. I had the best of both worlds. But still, there was that strange *philosophy,* that strange *perception.*

When had I first noticed it? That was no clearer to me than when I first noticed I had fingernails. It seemed always to have been there and it seemed always to have been a puzzle. It was in the air, like pollen. It affected everyone—the sense that femaleness was not as valuable as maleness. Nobody came right out and said it. Everybody just *knew* it.

That's why God was male and not female. That's why Adam was the original and Eve was created for him. That's why a woman was listed along with a man's other possessions in the Bible. That's why nobody in the Bible ever prayed for a woman child and always prayed for a man child. That's why some cultures still practiced female infanticide. There was something about maleness that was just . . . better. How had Aunt Mamie put it after that long talk we'd had? "Well, all I can say is that if a baby's going to be born, it's just better off if it's born a boy."

Except for that one area where femaleness *really* counts. Every girl is taught that one day the most wonderful of all things will happen. Her femaleness will be discovered by a man, desired by a man, and desperately needed by a man. He will need her *because* of, not in spite of, her femaleness. To be desired by a man transforms one's femaleness into something good. The bearing of children follows, that indispensable and thoroughly feminine marvel.

I was happy enough with that. But surely, *surely* there must be some way to explain that femaleness, in and of itself, counted as much.

What could I say tomorrow that would lift the women? Many of them would be perfectly happy people who were living exactly as they wanted to. But others would be suffering, consciously or unconsciously. Only last week I had sat by a woman at a banquet when the subject came up in our conversation and I had braved the question, "Do you think, when the answers are finally in, we will see that from God's point of view maleness is better than femaleness?"

She had stared at her plate for a moment, and then replied, "Well, I would hope that wouldn't be the case. But yes, yes, I think it will be." I was weary of conversations like that; weary of women sighing in resignation.

I would start my talk with the quote from Susa Young Gates, Brigham's daughter. She had written that her mother had exclaimed, upon finding out Susa's sex, "Shucks!" Aunt Zina had responded, "No, it isn't all shucks, it's wheat, and full weight too." That was a good image. I would build from there.

I had to be careful about what I said. It was easy to be labeled a heretic in talking about things like this, though most people had responded enthusiastically to *Daughters of Light*, the book I had published the year before. It was a compilation of the spiritual experiences of the early Mormon women. In all our telling of the wonderful experiences of the men, we had forgotten the women altogether and it was exciting to write of the healings, the revelations and the prophecies in which the women participated. I would use a few of those stories tomorrow. When I went downstairs Lynn Ann was just putting the third load of laundry into the dryer. As we walked together into the front room we saw it simultaneously, crayon marks all over the white wall beside the mirror. We both gasped.

"Emily!" I shouted. "John! Aaron!"

They came running, anxious to see what brought that exciting sound to my voice.

"Emily!" I pointed at the crayon marks. "Did *you* do this?" Emily haughtily folded her arms across her six-year-old body and glared at me. "Mama! If you see beautiful pictures drawn on the walls, you will know that I did them. If you see scribbles, you will know that the boys did them."

Behind me Lynn Ann dissolved into a great laugh. I struggled for a moment and then joined her. "Oh, that's wonderful," I said when I could catch my breath. "I can't wait to tell Gerald."

Gerald would probably call that night and he loved hearing all the wise, wonderful, and ridiculous things the children did and said.

After the children were in bed for their nap, I sat down to read *Women in Love* by D. H. Lawrence. Gerald had given it to me the previous week and had made me promise to have read it by the time he got back. But many of Lawrence's long, philosophical passages bored me mightily and there was something baffling about the two couples, particularly the mystical bond of the two men.

The last page. One of the men has been killed and the other is grieving deeply. Birkin's wife, Ursula, tries to comfort him.

> "Aren't I enough for you?" she asked.
>
> "No," he said. "You are enough for me, as far as a woman is concerned. You *are* all women to me. But I wanted a man friend, as eternal as you and I are eternal."
>
> "Why aren't I enough?" she said. "You are enough for me. I don't want anybody else but you. Why isn't it the same with you?"
>
> "Having you, I can live all my life without anybody else, any other sheer intimacy. But to make it complete, really happy, I wanted eternal union with a man too: another kind of love," he said.

"I don't believe it," she said. "It's an obstinacy, a theory, a perversity."

"Well," he said.

"You can't have two kinds of love. Why should you?"

"It seems as if I can't," he said. "Yet I wanted it."

"You can't have it, because it's false, impossible," she said.

"I don't believe that," he answered.

Slowly I put the book down and stared at the ceiling. Why was I hearing another voice in the voice of Birkin? Where was that strange chill coming from?

Gerald. Something . . . something about Gerald? Is that what Bobbie had said? Cold cut into my consciousness like the edge of an iceberg into an arctic sea. No. Not that. Of course not that. I got up quickly and put on a sweater and went into the kitchen to start supper.

It was always difficult to get through an evening cheerfully alone with the children. There were three of them and one of me. Gerald could joke them into anything. If a child started to cry Gerald would say, "Oh, no—your face is melting!" And the child could not refrain from laughing. I did not have that gift. I met the children straight on and sometimes it worked and sometimes it didn't. Tonight I could tell that my resources were low, so I tried not to ask too much of anyone.

"I'm going to work on my sculpture after supper, Mama," said Emily, happily playing with her green beans. "It's about you, Aaron, about you as a ti-ny, lit-tle baby. And you are going to be so cute!"

Last "family home evening" Gerald had given a lesson on art, and had made an assignment for each child to select something in the world that excited him or her and do something artistic with the idea—write a poem or a song or make a painting or a sculpture or a dance.

"Me too," said John. "I'm gonna paint a kitty!"

"What about you, Aaron?" I asked. "You going to have something ready for Daddy when he gets back? One of your great dances, hmm?"

"When Daddy coming home?" responded Aaron. He had already asked that several times today.

"In a few days. Pretty soon."

When the evening ritual of teeth and face and potty and drinks and prayers had been completed for each of the children, I remembered the last load of laundry. Had I said nine o'clock to Bobbie? She'd be here in just a few minutes. I picked up the laundry basket and took it into the front room. I could fold the clothes while we talked. From my pioneer roots I knew enough never to do one thing when I could do two. Bobbie wouldn't mind if I folded the laundry while we talked. I sat down and picked up a pair of Gerald's black socks, folding them the way he liked so that the elastic didn't stretch at the tops. I thought about calling to see how my father was. He had been in and out of the veterans' hospital and was making up his mind to die. We were trying to encourage him to fight, but he didn't see much point to it. That was strange to me. How could anyone not want to live?

The doorbell rang, and when I answered it, Bobbie said, "Hi," and quickly walked in and past me without looking at my face.

"Hi. Sit down."

She stood nervously for a moment, balancing on one foot, then the other. Then she sat down on the couch and looked at the rug.

"How are you?" I asked, going back to the wooden rocker and my laundry. My fingers felt an urgent need to involve themselves.

"Okay. I'm okay," she said quickly. "The kids? The kids all right?"

"They're fine."

Bobbie threw her head back, and then forward into her hands as if she were riding a bucking horse. After a moment she dropped her hands and looked at me. She was crying.

"Bobbie," I said quietly, "what's wrong?"

"Damn it!" She slammed her fist against the couch and then grabbed both knees. "He has no right to do this to you. No right!"

The edge of the iceberg pressed so hard I could barely breathe.

Crying and talking at the same time, she continued. "Maybe I shouldn't be here. I didn't know what to do. But . . . I *love you so much*. And it makes me *so damn mad. He has no right to do this to you!*"

I tried to form a question but no sound came out.

"I was in Salt Lake at The Sun—that's a place where gays get together. And Gerald was there. I couldn't *believe* it. I talked to him and he said that yes, he was gay, and that you knew he used to be but you didn't know that he still was. I didn't know what to do. Please don't hate me!"

She was staring at me, waiting for me to speak. Seconds, minutes went by.

"I'm sorry," she said quietly. "I'm sorry. Can I . . . do anything for you?"

Slowly I shook my head.

"Will you be all right?"

Slowly I nodded.

Bobbie stood up and ran out the door. There was the sound of her motorcycle in the driveway. There was the sound of the baseball crowd across the street, of a passing car, of crickets in the grass.

Slowly I stood up and stared for a minute or more at the pair of black socks in my hands. I reached down and put them back in the laundry basket, then made my way across the room, through the kitchen, down the basement stairs. I opened the door to Gerald's office, turned on the light and stepped in. The room smelled of him. The room was filled with him.

I sank onto the chair at the desk and reached for the card he had left with the telephone numbers on it. My fingers would not pick it up. I pressed it against the wood of the desk and slid it toward me. I picked up the telephone receiver and tried to dial. My finger could not find the numbers that were on the card. I hung up and pressed my hands together to stop their shaking. I had begun a little prayer as soon as Bobbie had started speaking. "Dear God, help me, help me," and it had stayed in my mind like a mantra. "Help me, help me." I leaned over the desk and pressed my forehead to the cool wood. Then I dialed again.

"Hello?" That was Mrs. Kruiswyck, whom Gerald had stayed with in Australia. She had never joined the Church, but she loved Gerald like a son.

"Trudy? This is Carol Lynn. Is Gerald there?"

"He is. We're having a wonderful visit. How are you, darling?"

"Fine. And you?"

"Wonderful! Here's Jerry."

"Hi, sweetheart. I was going to call you." A long pause. "Blossom? Are you there?"

"Gerald?" I could hardly hear my own voice. I'd have to speak louder. "Gerald?"

"Yes?"

"I have to ask you a question. Gerald, since you and I have been married, have there been any . . . men?"

Gerald's voice was low and tight when he finally spoke. "Yes. Yes, there have been."

A long pause. "Gerald? What do you want to do?"

"What?"

"Do you want to stay with us?"

"Blossom!" A world of pain was in Gerald's voice. "Oh, Blossom! Some questions don't even need to be asked."

"I'm asking."

"Of course I want to stay with you and the kids. Of *course* I do!"

"How?"

"Blossom, we can work it out." Gerald spoke firmly. "I've been trying to tell you. I've been preparing things so I could tell you. I feel awful that it happened like this. Please . . . just hang on until I get home. Please believe in me, believe in yourself, believe in us. We can find a way to work it out. Don't do anything, *anything* until I get home. Promise me that. Blossom?"

"Okay."

"What?"

"Okay."

"Blossom? I love you."

"I . . . love you too."

Both hands put the receiver back on the telephone. Slowly I crossed the room, turned out the light, closed the door, walked up the stairs, down the hall, and into the bathroom. I was shaking, shaking from the cold. I knelt down and turned on the water in the rub, only the hot water. I watched while the water filled the bathtub, while the steam rose and covered the walls and the mirror. Then I undressed and stepped into the tub. I shivered violently as the hot water met the chill of my feet and legs. Then I lowered myself into the water, feeling the heat travel upward to my neck and my chin. Still I shook.

The carillon bells on campus sounded the hour. Eight—nine—ten. And then I gave myself up to the moaning that rose in my throat in a primitive rhythm that made me hold myself and rock back and forth, back and forth to the strange, wounded sound of my own voice.

Chapter 6

The next morning Lynn Ann looked at me as if I had blood on my face.

"Carol Lynn! What's wrong?"

"I'm just tired. I didn't sleep much." That was not a lie. I hadn't slept at all. I had walked and rocked and lain down and gotten up and gone in to look at the children and picked Aaron up to hold because he was the smallest. Then, before they were to wake, I put a wet washcloth on my eyes. The world was still here and there were things to be done.

I had to move, I had to get ready to give a talk. Two hundred women would be waiting to hear me. One fulfills one's responsibilities. I could only move slowly. I got dressed and put on my makeup. I looked tired. Worse. Old. Worse. I looked ugly.

I was overwhelmed at how ugly I looked. How could I ever have thought I had nice eyes?

At the luncheon, I stared at the elegantly arranged flowers in the centerpiece as my introduction was given. It was a lie. It was all a lie. I was not the person they had invited to speak. I didn't even know who she was. I was a fraud. *They* thought I was an example of good Mormon womanhood. They were proud of me. I had a wonderful husband and three children and I wrote lovely poems. They didn't know anything. They didn't know that my eternal marriage was in ruins. They didn't know that my children's father was a homosexual. What if they knew that? They wouldn't want me then. They wouldn't ask me to speak then. Still, I would give my talk. I would speak on the wonderful world of women. In spite of the fact that my husband preferred men, I would tell them what a thrilling thing it is to be a woman. I didn't have a master's degree in drama for nothing. I could pull it off. I could lie once. And then I would never speak again. I would go home and cancel all the speaking engagements I had accepted. I would resign my seat on the Governor's Commission to plan the Bicentennial. I would cancel everything.

No one seemed to notice that I lied. Two hundred women applauded and many told me how much they'd enjoyed the speech and what an inspiration my writings were to them. I smiled and thanked them. If I could just get out the door and down the stairs, I would never, never have to do this again. How could they not know, I thought, as I finally opened the car door and sank into the driver's seat. I was saying the right words, and the right words were fine with them. Was that all they wanted? Is that all anybody wants, just to hear the right words?

On the way home I stopped in to visit my father whom I hadn't seen for a couple of days. Would he be able to tell?

"How is he?" I asked Gladys as she opened the door for me.

"He's not eating again, that's how he is," my stepmother replied, as if it were a personal affront. "That man is *so* stubborn!"

"Daddy?" I sat down beside his bed and touched his hand.

His eyes opened and he looked at me. "Hello, Sister."

"How are you feeling?"

"Not too good."

"Gladys says you won't eat."

He closed his eyes again and shook his head.

"I wish you would."

He made as firm a gesture as he could with his hands.

"Sister, I'm on my way out. If I could get better, I would. But I can't. Just leave me alone."

I took one of his hands and felt the tears come to my eyes. I didn't want him to be so frail, so helpless. But there was something else too. I felt relief. My father was going to die soon. He would never have to know what was happening to me. He would never have to know about Gerald. It would kill him. He had charged Gerald on our wedding day to take good care of me. *Oh, Daddy, die soon*, I thought. *And then you'll never have to know.*

And there was another thing I felt—I was envious of my father. *Envious!* He was going to die soon. He would be through with all of this. Wherever else there was, he would soon be there. *Oh, Daddy, if I did not have three children, I would lie down too. I would lie down and not eat or drink, and soon I would not be here.*

I let the children watch television all afternoon, something that never before had happened. I went upstairs to my room over the garage to try to think what to do. I had a dozen good friends I could call on for *anything*—anything except visiting upon them my enormous shame. I could tell no one.

If my house had been destroyed by fire, if my child had been run over I could call on the Church. The Church would be wonderful. But not this. I could not bear it. Gerald might be excommunicated and I would be humiliated and pitied.

Women with problems were encouraged to take them to the bishop or to the Relief Society president. I couldn't go to the bishop, not now. I had promised Gerald I'd do nothing until he got back.

And I *was* the Relief Society president. Women in the ward brought their problems to *me*. I had been amazed when the bishop called me to the job. "I'm not a Relief Society president!" I had protested. "I'm a maverick—I'm strange. I'm nothing *like* a Relief Society president!" But he had insisted I was the one for the job. He wanted to strengthen the compassionate service aspects of the Relief Society and he thought I was the one who could do it. Compassion, love, helpfulness. That's what it was all about. CHARITY NEVER FAILETH. That was our motto. What did it mean? Compassion. But not for wickedness. Not for the very lowest of the low. Not for . . . homosexuals.

I groaned aloud. How could this be happening to me? I had been doing everything right. I was keeping all my covenants. I had promised in the temple to be honest and chaste and to obey all the commandments. I was doing that. I prayed. We had family prayer. I paid my tithing. I went to all my meetings. We had family home evening once a week to teach the children to be faithful. Nothing like this was supposed to happen. Illness and accidents, maybe, and maybe financial problems. There was no shame in those. But not this, not something so shameful, so sinful you could not even speak it. I had thought it was over, done with, washed clean. I had been promised!

I went to my bookcase and pulled out the one book published by the Church that I knew had some mention of it, *The Miracle of Forgiveness* by Spencer W. Kimball. There it was in black-and-white. Homosexuality was "an ugly sin . . . repugnant . . . embarrassing . . . perversion . . . sin of the ages . . . degenerate . . . revolting . . . abominable and detestable crime against nature . . . carnal . . . unnatural . . . wrong in the sight of God . . . deep, dark sin." Under Mosaic law it carried the death penalty. Those words—those awful words—I had only pictured them as applying to someone so low, so evil and beastly that he hardly deserved breath. But they were talking about Gerald. Gerald!

I read on. "Satan incites the carnal man to ever-deepening degeneracy in his search for excitement until in many instances he is lost to any former considerations of decency.

Thus it is that through the ages, perhaps as an extension of homosexual practices, men and women have sunk even to seeking sexual satisfactions with animals."

The tears and the sobs came again. How could this be? Gerald was an unrepentant homosexual! Should I pack up the children and leave? Take them somewhere so he could never see them again? Where could I go?

I picked up the book and went on:

> After consideration of the evil aspects, the ugliness and prevalence of the evil of homosexuality, the glorious thing to remember is that it is curable and forgivable . . . if totally abandoned and if the repentance is sincere and absolute. Certainly it can be overcome, for there are numerous happy people who were once involved in its clutches and who have since completely transformed their lives. Therefore to those who say that this practice or any other evil is incurable, I respond: "How can you say the door cannot be opened until your knuckles are bloody, till your head is bruised, till your muscles are sore? It can be done. . . ."
>
> Many yielding to this ugly practice are basically good people who have become trapped in sin. They yield to a kind, helpful approach. Those who do not must be disciplined when all other treatments fail.
>
> Remember, the Lord loves the homosexual person as he does all of his other children. When that person repents and corrects his life, the Lord will smile and receive him.

Slowly I closed the book and put it down. It had not occurred to me, not once in all our married life, that Gerald had not completely and fully repented. What was it? Was it me? Was I not sufficiently attractive? Had I not been enough of a woman to make it work?

I stared at my hands and turned them over. They were small, a woman's hands. Was there something wrong with having a woman's hands? Were big hands better? Was there something wrong with having a woman's face? Woman's skin? Woman's breasts?

I sank to my knees and buried my face in the gray couch. *What's wrong with being a woman?* The cry came from the depths of me. Where could I go to find healing for the wound to the woman in me? Only to God. But . . .

Didn't God prefer men too, in a spiritual sense? God *was* male. God associated with males, did business with males, spoke to males, called males to his work. God did not transact important business with people with small woman's hands and a woman's face. He loved all of us, of course, but he preferred men. My mind moaned under the weight of it.

And God's Church preferred men. That was evident. Women were welcomed and respected and used, but not preferred. The hundred horror stories I had written out in my diary marched through my mind in sorry evidence. Only last month a rough cut of a film on Joseph Smith's early life had been shown to the Brethren. A scene at the kitchen table had panned the family group and ended on Lucy Mack Smith gazing devotedly at her son. One of the Brethren responded, "Why did that scene feature the mother? It should have featured the father. We're a priest-hood-oriented Church. We've got to feature the men. I'd like that scene shot over." No matter how many I heard, those stories hurt anew.

What's wrong with being a woman?

I had known all my life that somehow femaleness was second prize. But they had promised me, *promised* me that in this one thing I was safe. The man would want me, need me *because* I was a woman. My softer skin and woman's breasts would be indispensable. I had been cheated. I had been violated.

There must be some mistake. It could not be true that *everywhere I turned* they would rather I be male—not God and the Church and my husband too. I did not want to be a man. I liked being a woman. There must be some mistake, something I couldn't see, something no one had told me. I *will not accept this answer,* I cried inside. I *will beat my small woman's hands against heaven until I get a better answer!*

On the next day the anger came. I had slept just enough to find a little strength, and I woke up furious. The enormous, staggering betrayal washed over me in waves. *This must be what many of the early Mormon women had felt when they learned their husbands were being intimate with other women, or were planning to be,* I thought. To know that the person you love is sharing that most private act with other people! How could they bear it? How could I bear it? How dare Gerald do that to me? How dare he do it to us? How dare he let his filthy habits destroy all we had been working for in this life and in the world to come? How dare he do this to Emily? To John? To Aaron?

As I got out of bed my eye fell on *Women in Love.* How dare he give me that book? How dare he try to justify what he was doing? Damn D. H. Lawrence and his mystical male friendships. Damn Walt Whitman. And damn Gerald! I picked up *Women in Love* and walked quickly down the hall. At last I could walk quickly. I stood at the head of the stairs and threw the book down to the basement. It landed with a thud and skidded to the door of Gerald's office. Let him find it there. I was unused to thoughts of violence. I wouldn't let the children watch ugly things on television. But now there streamed through my mind images that shook me. In my mind I killed Gerald, I destroyed him utterly, I watched him suffer. I tore him and beat him and let him bleed.

No. I couldn't do that. I grabbed my mind and shook it. No, I would not have that. I would let nothing do that to me.

Another day to endure. Get dressed. Make breakfast. See Emily off to school. Find another answer if John asks again if I fell down and hurt myself. Go on.

When the visiting teachers rang my doorbell I was startled. I had forgotten that they had made an appointment for this morning. Once a month the visiting teachers went in pairs to call on all the women in the ward to give a short lesson and check on the welfare of the family. Good thing I had at least gotten dressed and combed my hair.

"Hi, Sister Pearson! How you doin'?" Why were newly married young women so cheerful? And this one in particular? Nancy never stopped bubbling.

"Fine. Come on in."

They entered and sat down on the couch. I pulled up the wooden rocker. As Relief Society president, I had paired up these two because I thought some of Nancy's effervescence might rub off on Lydia, a young single woman who was so shy one was almost afraid to speak loudly to her. She even seemed to hunch her shoulders if you hugged her so you couldn't get very close.

"Is everything going okay? The ward Relief Society president wants us to be sure to report any problems or needs."

I forced a laugh at that, and even Lydia smiled.

"We're fine," I said. "We're all fine."

Was that how it was, then? Did every woman in the ward who had a real heartbreak lie about it like I was lying? Did we need so badly to look as bright and happy as the perfect family on the front of the *Ensign,* the Church's official magazine, that we smiled no matter what the cost? Not everyone hid their hurts. I knew that. But I suddenly knew that many did. Too many.

We spoke of inconsequential things, of the beautiful colors up the canyon, of new twins in the ward, of a family moving to Arizona.

"Well," said Nancy, after a few minutes had passed, "the lesson this month is on faith. Again. It seems like we're always having lessons on faith, doesn't it? But maybe that's because we need them. At least I do. And Lydia's going to give the lesson."

Quietly, Lydia read a few thoughts from the manual and then talked a little about how she felt they applied. Good. I was glad to see her using her own words. That was a breakthrough. It was good for Lydia to have to speak, to have to get out of herself a little. Faith, she was saying, is walking to the very edge of the light and then taking a few steps into the darkness. We have to do it out of belief and courage, even though we can see nothing. We have to believe that the Lord will not desert us.

I sensed myself nodding my head. That was good. That was right. Even though we see only darkness we have to go on.

And even in the darkness we can comfort one another. And even though my visiting teachers came only once a month, even though they came because they were assigned to come, still they cared. If I could tell them, they would comfort me and pray for me. And even though I could not tell them, they still cared.

On the porch I hugged them both and thanked them for coming. And even though I still couldn't get very close to Lydia, I hugged her hard. What was her darkness? I wondered, I had wondered before, but I had never felt into her as I was doing now. It was as if my own wound was so raw and open that at the sight of another's pain I poured out, poured into her, wanted to heal her hurt with my own.

As I watched the two women walk down the sidewalk, I remembered Sister Loper. She was bedridden again and was scheduled to be taken to a rest home near her daughter in Oregon, but until next Friday she was the responsibility of the Relief Society. For the past few weeks I had made sure her visiting teachers were having food brought in and were tending to her basic needs. I had been to see her several times and decided to go again today.

As I walked up the cracked sidewalk of the little green frame house, I noticed the dried grass and weeds in the yard and made a mental note to see if we could get one of the youth groups in the ward to come over and do some watering and a little weeding. I knocked lightly on the screen door, then opened it and went in. "Sister Loper?"

"In here, Sister Pearson."

I turned to my left and entered a small bedroom. Even if I had not been there before, even if I had not had her voice to guide me, I would have found her by the rank odor that floated from the bedroom. I stepped into the room and looked at the tiny body on the bed. Pale blue eyes stared out from a weathered face topped by white hair cut in a man's style. Quickly I opened a window and stood as near to it as I could.

"How are you feeling today, Sister Loper?"

"Better. A little better." That's what my mother always said when she was dying of cancer.

"Can I . . . ?" I motioned to the bedside toilet.

"Oh, yes. Would you?"

Trying not to breathe, I took the little pan into the bathroom. As I emptied its contents into the toilet, I retched again and again. It felt oddly satisfying. It felt like something I had been trying to do for two days.

I rinsed out the pan and adjusted it again in its little chair.

"There," I said. "What else can I do?"

"Well, I hate to ask you, but the sisters hung out some laundry this morning. If you could bring it in?"

"Sure." The sheets and the towels had been in the sun for hours and I thought I had never smelled anything so wonderful. I stayed out longer than I had to with the white sheet pressed to my cheek. It was like medicine. It was a healing. That wonderful smell was a gift from God, a promise of health.

I stayed and talked for a while and gave Sister Loper a back rub, going gently over the little bones. Then I rubbed her feet. She smiled and closed her eyes. What a pitiful, helpless little thing.

Suddenly I remembered a statement Gerald had read to me a few weeks before. I was nearly asleep and he had shaken me and said, "Now listen to this, Blossom. Are you listening?"

"Mmm hmm." I had turned toward him and tried to open my eyes.

"This is from Alan Watts. 'The thing is to see in *all* faces the masks of God.' That's *it,* Blossom. That's what it's all about. If we can look at each other and *see everyone,* no matter who they are, as a manifestation of God, we've solved the puzzle!"

I looked at Sister Loper's tight little wrinkled face. A mask of God. Gerald was not talking about Sister Loper. He was talking about himself! That's why he spoke it so urgently. That's why he shook me and insisted that I hear it two or three times. If only he could make me see *all* faces, even *his* face, as a mask of God . . .

Waiting for the sound of the car in the driveway was excruciating.

"When will Daddy be here?" John asked, tearing through the kitchen with his truck. The children had asked that a dozen times already.

"Any time now. This afternoon. That's all I know." Gerald had decided, instead of rushing right home to meet the crisis, to stay and go to the workshop. It might be part of the solution, he reasoned. If he could make some of these psychic-spiritual breakthroughs he'd been working on, perhaps he could see better his own situation, our situation, and what it all meant. Besides, staying away for a few days would give me a little time to recover before we saw each other.

One week. Had it only been one week? Years had gone

faster. I had confided in no one, only gone over it and over it with myself.

> Can you become
> Acclimated to pain?
> Can the shiver cease?
> And some condition
> Almost comfortable set in?
> The polar bear has been so long a resident
>   of frost
> That the ice he walks barefoot
> Is not reported to the brain.
> Can you become
> Acclimated to pain?

I washed the kitchen cupboards as I listened for the car. Physical work was the only kind I'd been able to do for a week. Hands can move no matter what.

"I'm so glad when Daddy comes home," Emily sang from the front room. "Glad as I can be—"

Please, Emily. Please don't sing that song again, I begged silently, as I leaned over the counter and closed my eyes! The children had sung it in Sunday School on Father's Day a few months ago.

Gerald had beamed as he'd watched his three little angels singing to him.

"I'll pat his cheek and give him what?" Emily sang on. "A great, big kiss!"

"Emily!" I called sharply. "John! Aaron!"

The three came running.

"Listen. Will you please go out on the front lawn and wait for Daddy out there? Here's a popsicle."

The popsicles did it. Happily the three children trudged out front to watch for Daddy. Why did I need so badly to be alone? Would I ever again have enough energy to have three children in the same room with me?

When I heard the sound of the car I had to take hold of the sink for a moment. I always knew when Gerald was home because he revved the motor a little before turning off the ignition. He said it made the car easier to start the next time you used it. There it was. The motor, the rev, the slam of the door, the shrieks of the children.

I lifted a corner of the curtain and looked out the window.

I had opened none of the drapes for a week. Emily was in Gerald's arms. Then John and Aaron. They helped him lug his suitcase and his briefcase up the porch stairs. I straightened up beside the sink. If I could just keep the blood moving through my veins I would not keel over. I breathed deeply a few times, the way Sister Pardoe had taught me to do against stage fright. Fill the abdomen.

"Where's Mom?"

"In the kitchen. I finished my sculpture, Daddy. Do you want to see it?"

"In a minute."

Gerald walked into the kitchen. It was just . . . Gerald. He had done it hundreds of times before. It was just Gerald walking into the kitchen. I looked at him and listened to my voice say, "Hi, Gerald."

"Hi, Blossom."

We looked at one another, tentative, questioning.

"Emily's sculpture's real good, Daddy. And so's my kitty," said John. "You want to see them?"

"Daddy, did Mommy tell you what the *boys* did on the wall?"

"Emily," I said, "go turn on *Sesame Street*, would you please? We'll be out in a few minutes."

"Oh, all right," she said, and stomped off to the front room, followed by her brothers.

Gerald picked up his suitcase and walked down the hall. I followed him. I shut the door to our bedroom and watched Gerald put his suitcase down beside the closet. Then he turned around and looked at me.

The thing is to see in all faces the masks of God.

And then we were in each other's arms, sobbing, pressing against each other and against the monumental mystery that lay between us and around us, that I knew would be there for the rest of our lives.

Chapter 7

Had I been able to hate Gerald, it would have been simpler. I tried to let it happen and it would not. I watched him as we went through the rest of the day waiting for evening when we could be alone and talk. He appeared to be *the same person* that I had been living with for eight years. Was it possible?

At supper he told the children silly stories of things he had seen on his trip and made them laugh. "And there's this grimy little bag lady that's on the same corner every night in San Francisco. She wears old slippers and doesn't have many teeth and she goes around singing as loud as she can, "Gonna wash my back tonight—hallelujah—gonna wash my back tonight—hallelujah!"

Was it possible that an unrepentant homosexual could still love his children? Or was I going a little mad? Was Satan making his first inroads against my sense of right and wrong? Should I even have let Gerald in the house? But there he was, *the same person* I had loved all these years. He was a little anxious. I could see that. But his light still shone. It had not gone out. Gerald had sold out to Satan. *Why didn't it show?*

When finally Emily's sculpture and Johnny's kitty and Aaron's rendition of "If You Chance to Meet a Frown" had been properly admired and the children had been put to bed (the children were to see nothing wrong; at all costs the children were to see nothing wrong), Gerald and I sat down on the couch and looked at each other.

"How was the workshop?" I asked quietly.

Gerald gave a short laugh. "I had diarrhea the whole time, from the moment of your phone call. Have you ever tried to have an out-of-the-body experience while you've got diarrhea?"

"No, I haven't. Sorry I spoiled your fun."

"Blossom." Gerald reached over and took my hand. I let him.

"Please don't be caustic with me. You have such a way of being caustic when you want to. Please don't."

I stared at the floor and said nothing.

"I want to tell you everything," Gerald went on. "Everything. And I will answer every question you have. Please try not to judge. Please try just to listen."

Gerald thought a moment, and then went on. "I was not being dishonest with you when we married. I loved you. You were wonderful and I really did love you. I thought that the *problem* would be taken care of. They told me it would be. I did everything they said to do. And I thought for a few months that everything was changed."

"But, Gerald," I interrupted, "we were—I was—happy!"

"And I was too, in many, many ways. Blossom, this is not your fault. Maybe you think it is, but it has nothing to do with you, only with me. Yes, we were happy. I liked being with you. I even liked being with you physically. But to me it was like, like we were such good friends that we shared everything with each other, even sex. It was never quite like, like lovers. There is this other thing in me, Blossom, and it has never gone away and I know now that it never will. There is this thing in me that needs, that *insists* that my strongest feelings be for a man. It is a need that seems to be

78

as deep in me as my need for food and breath. I tried to beat
it to death, to strangle it, to smother it. And it has not died.
Blossom, I know the anguish you've been through this last
week. Can you understand that I have been in anguish too?
And for more than a week."

"Gerald," I said, "it's *wrong*."

"Wrong!" Gerald put his face into his hands and then
looked up. "I have taken that word and used it like a whip
on myself. I have flagellated myself with that word until I'm
bloody. But it does not change things. I have fasted, I have
prayed. How many thousands of prayers I have prayed! And
it does not change things. If my homosexuality is wrong,
then *I* am wrong, the fact of my *being* is wrong. Because
that's what *I am!*"

"When did you finally know?"

"About a year after we married."

"Did you . . . meet someone?"

"No. I just knew. Inside me. And I can tell you the exact
moment. You won't remember this. It was Sunday morning
and I turned on the program of poetry reading on KSL. 'The
Buried Life' by Matthew Arnold. My own life, my buried
life, came washing over me, drowning me. I just lay there
and sobbed. 'Tricked in disguises, alien to the rest of men,
and alien to themselves.' That was me. An alien. Disguised.
Trying to give my all to being something that I really was
not. An alien, trying to find home."

I heard all the words. The language was not foreign, but
the sense was foreign. I felt we could continue to talk forever
and I would still miss the sense of it. I had to take a deep
breath before I could ask the next question.

"Gerald, when did you first . . . ?"

"Act on those feelings?"

I nodded.

"On the tour to Europe."

"While I was home, pregnant with your child?" I cried,
remembering that "friendship ring," finally understanding

79

it. "While I was pregnant, you and your roommate . . . all over Europe—"

"He wasn't my roommate."

"You and whoever were—" Angrily I stood up and walked away from the couch. "Why didn't you tell me before you went?" I whirled around to look at Gerald. "Why didn't you say, 'Look, we've made a terrible mistake. I can't keep my promises. Let me go!' Why didn't you say that to me?"

The hurt in Gerald's eyes was huge. "Because I never really thought it *was* a terrible mistake. In spite of this, we've had one of the best marriages I've known. I didn't want to leave you. And then Emily and the boys. How could I leave them? Maybe I should have come to you and said let's end it, but I couldn't bear that. I decided maybe the best answer was just to let my buried life breathe from time to time. I thought maybe you would never have to know, never have to be hurt." Gerald heaved a long sigh and leaned back. "I found out it doesn't work that way. I hate not being honest. I hate it. I knew I'd have to tell you. I've been trying to. Oh, Blossom, you can't imagine how many of the things I have said over the last several years have had one goal in mind—to prepare you to accept me as I really am."

"Accept you?"

"Accept me. Look past the horror you've been conditioned to and really *see* me. Love me. And, if you can, stay with me."

"*How?* Gerald, what you're asking is crazy! I don't know any woman who could be in a marriage like that. You want *everything?*" Then it hit me, the memory of Gerald and Paul and me, in the car, close together, Gerald holding my hand. How cruel! To both Paul and me. That was the kind of life Gerald wanted?

"You could do it if you wanted to," Gerald said.

"I *don't* want to," I cried. "I don't want to and I couldn't if I did. It is not in me, and I'm glad it isn't because the whole thing is wrong!"

Gerald shook his head and spoke as if to himself. "Wrong."

"Listen, Gerald. You can change. I know you can. If you want to stay with us badly enough, if you want to make things work. Now that it's out in the open we'll work on it together. We'll get help, through the Church, through counseling."

Tears of frustration filled Gerald's eyes and he clenched his fists.

"Counseling! Oh, Blossom, I have had all I want of the Church's counseling. Before I went on my mission, I went again and again to the Church's top expert on this subject. He's a good man, a kind and loving man, but he does not even begin to understand the depth of the homosexual condition. He told me I would be all right if I would just continue in fasting and prayer and *not touch myself when I went to the bathroom.*"

"But there must be other treatments, professional treatments."

Gerald nodded his head and he looked tired and old. "And nobody I have ever known has gotten anything from the treatments but more guilt and more hopes smashed. Like Sam. Let me tell you about Sam. No. I want you to meet him. I want you to hear his story from himself. Will you?"

I didn't want to meet Sam or hear about treatments that didn't work. But I said I would meet him. If I was going to fight this thing, I had to know what I could about the enemy. We got ready for bed as we had how many hundreds of times.

"Do you . . . do you still want to pray?" I asked.

"Blossom, do you really think that homosexual people don't pray? Of course I still want to pray."

We knelt and Gerald offered the prayer as he had now many hundreds of times.

"And we're grateful for the love we share. Please bless us that during these difficult times we don't lose sight of that.

I'm so grateful for Carol Lynn and for her goodness. Please bless her that her pain will be lightened. Help us to find answers to our problems. And bless the children that they will not be hurt."

I managed to find enough voice to say "Amen."

A few evenings later in Gerald's office, a short, dark, nice-looking young man held out his hand, "Hi, I'm Sam. I've heard a lot about you."

"Hi, Sam."

I would not have known he was gay. We shook hands, then sat down on the floor, leaning against the giant corduroy cushions Gerald had made for his meditation classes.

"Sam knows why he's here, Blossom. Go ahead, Sam; let's hear the story of your life."

"The story of my life. Oh, boy. Got any hidden microphones around here?"

When Gerald laughed, Sam went on. "I've got nothing to hide. Salt Lake's got a file on me this thick. They know *everything*. I was born in Provo, just up the hill a little ways. Very Mormon family. My dad's been a high councilman as long as can remember. I grew up a good little Mormon boy, put money in the bank to go on a mission, knew I'd get married and have good little Mormon kids. I mean, *I wanted to.* I really wanted to, but I could tell by junior high that something was wrong. Emotionally I was a mess. I didn't know why. I talked to my school counselor and he said he couldn't help me but he sent me to somebody. I spent months going to this guy in the city's mental health offices, and he told me he thought I was a homosexual. I didn't even know what that was. Well, I knew that guys turned me on and girls didn't, but I hadn't *done* anything. If this guy said I was a homosexual, then I guess I was. And I figured I was the only one in the Rocky Mountains, at least in the state of Utah."

Gerald laughed again.

"So I asked if he could cure me and he said he would try. I went in every week and we talked about me and about my family and he gave me some mental exercises to do. Nothing was happening and we both knew it. So he sent me to somebody else who sent me to somebody else, and by the time I was out of high school I was a bigger mess than ever."

"Did your family know?" I asked.

"Nothing. I made sure they knew nothing. No way could they have dealt with it. I paid for my therapy by working after school. I figure that by the time I finished college I had paid about fifteen thousand dollars out of my own pocket trying to find the cure. And my parents never knew. They know now. This last year they've known." Sam's large brown eyes became wistful. "But I wanted so bad to be *cured* and get married and do everything they wanted me to do."

Fifteen thousand dollars? Sam had raised fifteen thousand dollars after school raking leaves or shoveling snow or loading trucks so he could find the cure for a problem he never asked for? And he had protected his parents all those years? It was not fair.

"When I went to BYU," he continued, "I talked to my bishop. He worked with me and also sent me to the campus counseling office. And they said that besides all the usual spiritual approaches and traditional counseling, they were using a thing that they had high hopes for, aversion therapy, electric shock therapy. I talked to some guys who were doing it, and one of them thought maybe it was helping, but I still wasn't crazy about the idea. And all this time I was going up to Salt Lake to have my interviews with the Brethren. The one I met with insisted homosexuality is caused by masturbation, and if I could just 'conquer the habit,' I wouldn't be a homosexual anymore."

"Sam," I interrupted, "are you making this up?"

"Not one word. I swear, not one word. Eventually I got desperate," Sam went on. "Mom and Dad kept talking about my mission and asked if I was preparing to go. I wanted to go. I always loved the Church and believed in it, but I knew I couldn't go like I was. So I went back to BYU counseling and said I would do the shock therapy." Sam took a deep breath and blew it out slowly. "Oh, boy. Sorry. I get jumpy just thinking about it."

I stared at him, horrified. "What did they *do*?"

Sam spoke slowly, reliving the experience. "They strapped me in a chair and attached wires to me. Then they showed me porno movies of men in sexual activity. When I got turned on, they gave me a shock. At first it was just a tiny shock on one finger, then all five fingers, and then both hands. After that they added my forearms, and then my calves and thighs. That was when they started cranking up the voltage. I had to go in two or three times a week. They figured if you associated pain with homosexual sex, you wouldn't want it anymore. And then they would show the same kinds of pictures of women without the shock, so that *that's* what you'd start to want. Only it didn't work. All I wanted was not to touch anybody, not to be with any-body. I felt like I was being turned into a zombie. I would walk down the street and be freaked by everyone. The idea of touching *anyone,* even my family, made me sick. But I thought maybe after the next session it'd start to work. Maybe then I could look at a girl and want to touch her. So I made myself . . ." Sam closed his eyes and clenched his fists. "I made myself walk up those steps and go into that build-ing and sit down in that chair. *And take the shocks.* Until I gave up. One day I stood outside the door and I could not stop shaking enough to walk in. There were burns on my arms. But inside there was nothing different. Nothing! Just more pain. More disappointments. More guilt. So I turned around and I left and I never went back."

We were all three silent for a moment. Then I asked, "What are you going to do now?"

Sam shrugged his shoulders. "Just live. Just live the best I can. My folks know and they're slowly adjusting to the idea. I've been seeing another therapist, a man in Salt Lake, a non-Mormon. My first time there he said, 'I can't promise you any changes. All I can do is help you decide for yourself what you really want and how you can get it.' He's been helpful. I don't hate myself anymore. I'm a homosexual person and I'm working on liking myself. I can't do it in Utah, and I can't do it in the Church. Next month I'm moving to Los Angeles."

I watched as tears formed in Sam's eyes and he brushed them away.

"Damn!" he said. "I wasn't going to— It's . . . John. He was going to come with me to Los Angeles. We weren't lovers or anything, just friends. He'd been through just about everything I had, even the shocks. We were going to drop everything and go make a new life. He told that to the General Authority that was on his case, and the man told him he'd be better off at the bottom of the Great Salt Lake with a millstone tied around his neck than to stay a homosexual. John believed him. He believed everything they said to him. He drove back to Provo, told his roommates he was going to the laundromat, drove up Rock Canyon, laid out a blanket, and blew his brains out."

"But, Sam, the Brethren don't want them to commit *suicide*. Of course they don't!"

"Blossom," Gerald spoke to me as if he were very tired. "Do you know how many young men in these valleys have killed themselves because they had been made to feel that they were *so low* they did not deserve to breathe? Because men whose voices they took to be the voice of God told them that if they could not change, their souls were forever lost? And they *could not change*."

Could not? Why would God ask something if it could not be done? And where *was* God in all this anyway?

"Sam," I said, "among all of the gay men that you know, do you know any, *any* that through any kind of therapy have changed?"

85

Sam shook his head. "I could name two dozen who have tried as hard as I have and *not* changed. And I could name several who married just like Gerald did in the hope that would take care of it. One is still hanging in there, but I know he's very shaky. I could name two who want to stay in the Church so bad that they've decided to try to be celibate the rest of their lives, but inside they're just the same. And I could name half a dozen older married men who are leading double lives. Maybe somewhere there's the miracle case, the miracle cure, but I don't know where it is."

This was not what I wanted to hear. I didn't feel that Sam was lying to me, or that Gerald was either, but there *must* be some success stories somewhere. Was it possible that nobody really had the answers? Maybe there was more to it than that it was just a *sin*. Maybe it *was* a real condition not of their choosing. But where was free agency in all of this? And if it was caused by something outside of their control, were they sinners or *sinned against?* Maybe the Brethren in Salt Lake were just as baffled as I was. Maybe the counselors who strapped electrodes to the bodies of gay men were also flailing around in the dark for answers. Here were all these young men who did not fit the pattern that the Brethren *knew* was the only true pattern. Maybe *this* will work. Maybe *that* will work. Oh, but to let well-meaning counselors send shocks through their bodies! To tell them they'd be better off at the bottom of the Great Salt Lake!

Gerald had been planning a surprise party for my birthday, but he decided to tell me about it. "I figure you've had enough surprises for a while. Do you feel like having a party, or should I cancel it?"

I thought for a moment. "Let's have the party. I deserve a party."

I was on the verge of tears all night, but I smiled. Once I had a Sunday School teacher who had been in a terrible accident and had a headache for the rest of his life. It never left him. But he always smiled. Is this how it will be, I wondered, until I die? I will just make myself smile?

Something happened at the birthday party. I began to remember that I was a person, that I had been born a little girl in 1939 and that I had lived for a long time before I even met Gerald. In spite of my devotion to the cause of women retaining an individuality of their own, in spite of my successful career, somehow I had let it happen to me, that sliding into my husband's shadow. Our house reflected more of him than it did of me. Even the kitchen. Our conversations were more focused on his interests than on mine. Gerald, for all his goodness, was always at the center of attention. He wanted to be. I had therefore taken second place.

"Being married to Gerald is a spectator sport," I had once joked. He was so interesting, so intense, that I loved watching him. But something of me had been lost along the way.

I looked at the thirty-five candles on the cake. Eight of them were years with Gerald. Twenty-seven were years without him, years with family and friends, sharing experiences, work, fun. I didn't even know who Gerald was anymore, and so I didn't know who I was. But I used to know. I used to be a person who existed all by myself without leaning on anybody. No matter what Gerald was or was not, I was still a person in my own right. I had myself, my children, my work, and friends who loved me and sang "Happy Birthday" and played charades because it was my favorite game. Mine, not Gerald's.

When they were gone and we had cleaned up in silence, I asked Gerald to sit down.

"Thanks for the party," I said.

"I wish I could give you more than a party, Blossom. I wish I could give you everything you deserve."

"Gerald, I know what you're hoping for, but I can't do it. I am not capable of sustaining a marriage under the circumstances you want. I can only be in a marriage where there's sexual fidelity. Even if this were the regular up-front polygamy instead of a strange version sneaked in the back door, I would not be able to manage it. I am a monogamist. I am the person who wrote on polygamy when Dr. Clark assigned 'A Fate Worse Than Death.' You have your limits and I have mine. I cannot do it."

A cheer erupted from the ballpark across the street. I smiled weakly. "Thank you very much," I said. "See, Gerald? They don't want me to either."

"Look, Blossom, let's not make any rash decisions right now. I'll make you a bargain. For the time being I will put away my other needs. All of them. I promise. I know I can't do that forever, but I will for a while. And during that time I want you to try to see things from my point of view. I want you to learn about homosexuality. I don't want you to throw me out until you understand me. Will you do that?"

I thought for a moment. "Okay. I can do that."

Chapter 8

It was strange to add a study of homosexuality to my study for *The Flight and the Nest,* the book I was writing on Mormon pioneer women. But I was a pioneer. I had been thrust onto a bizarre frontier where no one had traveled before. Reason told me it could not be possible that no woman had ever before found herself on the same ground, but that did me little good. I felt I was alone. The plains stretched endlessly. There were no markers, no sun-bleached buffalo skulls with friendly messages on them left by the party just ahead.

I was fourth-generation Mormon and many of my ancestors had come to Utah before the railroad. *How could they have survived*, I wondered. How could they have gone out and met the blizzards and the blistering heat and the wolves and the Indians? My grandmother Sarah had walked twelve hundred miles when she was eight and had seen her sister laid in a shallow grave along the way. My great-grandfather Thomas had marched with the Mormon Battalion in the fight against Mexico and had boiled and eaten his leather shirt to avoid starvation. But I wondered now if maybe, given a choice, I would take their trials rather than my own. A blizzard was a respectable enemy. You did what you could and then took the consequences. Hunger was something you could do battle with and often outsmart. Twelve hundred miles was a long way, but you just put one foot in front of the other again and again.

Where was my adversary? In which direction lay the Promised Land? I had no hint where to move or when. For a time, until I shared the burden with a woman who was very close to me, my only companion was Gerald, my enemy and my best friend.

It was not hard to love Gerald again, or to love him still. Our sorrows were not of his will, and that knowledge gave me enough energy to feel that surely we could find a solution. Surely we could work a miracle.

Within a couple of months we were living in all ways as husband and wife. There was the constant, dull pain but the momentum of life continued. We could even laugh from time to time and play Authors again and have private jokes. Maybe if I could just not think about it, it would dissolve, by itself.

But Gerald was making me think. He gave me a book written for families of gay people. Much of it made sense, but midway through I became very uncomfortable.

"I can't read this," I said, handing the book back to Gerald. "Whoever wrote this is as zealous as a Mormon missionary. I think he'd like to turn *everybody* gay."

I knew so little to start, only that homosexual love had been accepted and even idealized in ancient Greece. As I read, I learned that "faggots" had been burned at the stake along with witches in medieval Europe and that homosexual people have a three-thousand-year history as criminals, suffering fines, public humiliation, imprisonment, exile, torture, castration, and stoning. Under the Third Reich, 250,000 homosexuals were rounded up, forced to wear pink triangles, and exterminated in Nazi concentration camps.

I began to look at all the wildly conflicting theories about the development of homosexuality. Nobody agrees. One expert says it's an emotionally arrested state of development caused by something in the relationship with the parents, usually an emotionally absent father and a devouring mother. Somebody else says it's a full-fledged psychosis. Several authorities claim that most cases have a genetic, or biological, base; others are certain that homosexuality is caused by experimentation that becomes habitual, or a lack of adult role models of the appropriate sex, or fear and mistrust of the opposite sex, or rejection of the societal role of one's gender. A large number of investigators insist the condition is not pathological at all, but another variant of nature, which also makes people right-handed and left-handed and blue-eyed and brown-eyed, and that the only *problem* with it is the problem society makes by not accepting it. Another writer suggests that homosexuality is caused by the prevailing attitude that women are inferior, noting that the Romans insisted that sex with men is superior because men are superior.

I had to smile at that one. A bitter smile. Why not? It was as good as any other theory I'd read. There was all that stuff in the air that everybody breathed that said maleness was better than femaleness. Maybe that, along with other factors, settled in some subconscious minds and translated into sexual preference for men.

"All right, Gerald," I said one day. "Give me your theory. What causes homosexuality?"

"Well, a lot of gay people would answer that by saying, 'What causes heterosexuality?' but I think there's more to it than that. I think that somehow it's life rebelling against the rigid masculine position that men have been forced into. Men are so combative, so competitive, and so tough—at least that's what society asks of them. Maybe we've created a backlash to question all that."

"But, Gerald, why are there *two opposites*? Why does life itself depend on two opposites? If everybody were homosexual—"

"Life will always insist on procreation, but maybe life wants to free a certain segment of the population for *other* kinds of creating. Homosexual people have always been among the most productive artists, you know."

"Well then, if it's so honorable, why is the whole thing conducted in the dark? Why do homosexual men do such strange things? Why do they meet one another in bathrooms?"

"Where can they meet one another? Do you think that's their first choice? Public bathrooms? The little homosexual boy is told, 'No! You can't do that!' He has to hide what he feels or be punished, but his feelings can't stay bottled up forever. So they find strange, pitiful expressions. Don't you think gay people would rather date like everybody else—out in the open?—hold hands in church and meet in acceptable places? Maybe that's one reason why some gays are so promiscuous, why sex becomes a fixation with them instead of a normal part of their lives. Look, don't try to get me to say there is no sickness in much of the gay lifestyle. There is a lot that's unhealthy. But is it from being gay? Or from being persecuted? As I judge it, Blossom, the whole matter of sexuality is a question of what is life giving and what is not. All relationships should be judged that way. In the processes of life, which are life promoting and which are death promoting?"

Our conversation on the subject was laid down and picked up again like a piece of embroidery. Like embroidery it became more complex. Innumerable threads criss-crossed the underside, linking this and that and forming strange patterns. I would lay it down and shake my head, thinking, well, he's right on this and this and this, but he's still *wrong*. The whole thing is still *wrong*.

When I discovered in January that I was pregnant, I was amazed. This was definitely not in the game plan, certainly not with things as shaky as they were.

Gerald shook his head and half smiled. "I knew it. I knew she was so stubborn we could not stop her."

"What?"

"A couple of months ago as I was meditating downstairs, I sensed this presence, this female presence, and she was there to let me know that she was going to join our family. I told her no, that she was definitely not invited, at least not now, and she so much as told me that she was coming anyway."

"But this is a terrible time," I said. "We don't even know what's going to happen to us."

"Blossom, what you and I got into together is not over yet, and I don't think it ever will be. We've still got some work to do together. Obviously one part of it is that stubborn little creature that just sneaked into the picture. Hang on, kiddo." Gerald laughed. "We're not through yet!"

I continued to smile at Relief Society, and despite the pain, it wasn't always fake. There is a blessing in the things that have to be done. Make sure there are enough baked potatoes for the ward dinner. Make sure the children have enough clean clothes. Make sure that after supper Daddy hears a chapter of the book I'm reading to him. Make sure Sister Benson has meals brought in for a week after her surgery. Make sure that we have enough money in the bank for the house payment. That one was not easy. Gerald's romantic idealism was evident not only in his personal life but in his business management as well. I urged him to go slow on new products, but with his characteristic enthusiasm and faith, he produced two record albums. I balanced my reservations with my belief that Gerald could miraculously make it work, and I supported him in the venture. The albums were not successful and soon we were in serious financial straits. Gerald worked day and night to try to make the company solvent, and I gave all my energies to keeping the family afloat. Soon it was apparent that we should sell the house and use the money to pay business debts. We would give our books to other publishers and close down our company.

I accepted all the work that came my way from the BYU motion picture studio. I accepted a commission to write the text to a new choral symphony by Crawford Gates. It would be Utah's major offering of the Bicentennial and would feature the first joint appearance of the Mormon Tabernacle Choir and the Utah Symphony Orchestra. I was preparing a new book of poems and a musical play for children called *My Turn on Earth.*

And I continued research for my book on Mormon pioneer women. I had to do that; it was what fed *me,* gave me the energy to get up in the morning. Maybe in my own strange marriage, being female would continue to come in second. But there were hundreds of thousands of women in more conventional situations who also were getting second prize. My friend Ruth had recently challenged her husband on all the things that she felt uncomfortable about. "What would you do," she asked him, "if you had to be the woman in this marriage?—if I had been born the man and you the woman?" He had thought a moment and then said, "Well, I guess I'd just make the best of a bad deal." How *dare* he say that? How *dare* the human family conspire to make being a woman a bad deal?

My first book on Mormon women had dealt with their receiving and exercising spiritual gifts. The book I was currently working on would show what Mormon women were saying a hundred years ago on "the woman question," especially in their newspaper, *The Woman's Exponent.* I had first found some copies of the paper when Aunt Mamie had taken me up to Dingle, Idaho, to the old family home. The search expanded, and I discovered that my pioneer foremothers questioned the status of women in terms stronger than my sisters today would ever dare to. They sang suffrage songs and held suffrage meetings and called Susan B. Anthony "humanity's uncrowned queen." Emmeline B. Wells, who edited the paper for forty years, labored unceasingly for every educational, professional, and political opportunity for women, even lauding the idea of a woman president of the United States. Brigham Young sent women back East to become doctors of medicine and encouraged them in other professions.

In my next book of poems, I dealt with the subject too, including in the volume a long narrative poem about a friend's mother, who did everything for everybody and nothing for herself and who bought a red dress but never wore it. I also wrote about stewardship. I had overheard Gerald saying, "If it's true that the Lord has placed me over Carol Lynn as her steward, then my job is to make sure she becomes everything she can become, or I will have to account for it."

Maybe I would continue to avoid mirrors for the rest of my life and never know what it feels like to have the woman in me really desired. But against the centuries-old consciousness that made women less, I could do battle.

I savored the small victories. Sister Lindgren's husband was our home teacher (priesthood representative of the bishop) and I had been educating him on how subtly we discount women. Finally it had dawned on him that without meaning to, he had been treating his wife like a child. He had apologized to her and was behaving differently. *The Flight and the Nest* was well received, and the Church's public communications office sent me to New York for media interviews as a Mormon woman who had important things to say. The poems, "Millie's Mother's Red Dress" and "The Steward" and others, were widely used. I went to Mexico, seven months pregnant, for the International Woman's Year meeting, and heard thousands of my sisters from every nation discuss from their own points of view the concerns of women. I had no money to go, but my good brother Warren bought me a plane ticket.

It was during this period that my father was dying. We brought him over to our house in March because his wife Gladys could no longer lift him. Gerald could pick him up and put him in the bathtub and lift him out again. I watched Daddy grow weaker and weaker and I sat for hours by his bed trying to penetrate the final mystery. What did I know anymore? Just that we keep breathing until our bodies finally say no. And that we use that breath to fight with, to figure out some way to lift the human condition, to eat good fresh food for those who are on their way in, and to hold the hands of those who are on their way out.

Daddy died in March and Katy was born in September.

Gerald was in the delivery room and again he held my legs and told me I was doing great. It was a girl, that stubborn little female Gerald had anticipated, a charming creature who brought me days of endless delight. I had prayed for a girl because I knew there must be a lot of them left over from when people prayed only for a man-child.

I was the one who suggested the move from Utah to California. Maybe I started thinking about it the Saturday morning of the Stake Relief Society "Parade of Weddings" program. Each stake (a geographical unit that embraces a number of wards) had been asked to create a program with a historical theme to celebrate the Bicentennial. I received the directive from the Stake Relief Society president that the stake board had decided on a wedding theme, commemorating the weddings of all the women in the eight wards that comprised our stake. Each ward was to mount a display of wedding pictures and paraphernalia, and as many women as still could were to model their wedding dresses in a fashion show.

I was stunned. Here we have an opportunity to do something wonderful—maybe to pay tribute to those grand women of our pioneer past—and we're going to muster the same energy that we used to make the desert blossom as the rose and turn it all to a morning to reminisce about our *weddings*. I would have raised my hand with alternate suggestions had I been involved. "What about our single sisters, or those who are divorced?" I would have asked. And I would have thought, *What about me?*

It was very odd. I took out my wedding dress. I was still Relief Society president and I had to lead out. I hauled out the wedding pictures and the little white candy swan that had been one of the decorations on our cake and helped to arrange them in the display. We had a glass case for the really valuable things. There were the hundred-year-old ivory leather boots, worn by Sister Sampson's grandmother at her wedding and an exquisite lace dress worn by Sister Harris when she married fifty years before. There were elegant hair combs, faded garters, delicate handkerchiefs, jewelry, picture albums, wedding portraits, dress forms on which were pinned wedding gowns of all styles, new and old.

It was beautifully done, but I stared at the glass cases as I would stare at caskets. How many of those hopes and promises, how much of that youthful, innocent joy had been fulfilled?

Because of my Church position I knew there were women there whose marriages were sources of great joy; but there were others who cried in despair several times a week, though they brought their happy wedding pictures and homemade garters for the display.

The music started. That was our cue to go to the dressing room and get ready for the "Parade of Weddings" fashion show. Everyone who could still fit into her wedding dress was expected to wear it and be introduced, cross the stage, turn around, and smile. How strange to pull the white satin over my shoulders, to wear again the crystal bodice I had bought in Mexico those ten years ago, and to arrange the veil. I could do it. I had been in dozens of plays. You put on the costume and the makeup and you play your part. Today's play was called, "My Happy Wedding."

The "Hawaiian Wedding Song" was playing as I stepped onto the stage. "And shimmering into the spotlight now is Sister Carol Lynn Pearson of the Bonneville Ward in a stunning dress that features a crystal bodice handmade in Mexico. Besides writing her lovely poems, Sister Pearson is an example to us all with her darling husband and those four darling children."

I almost laughed. It felt like those times I used to get the giggles during the sacrament when I was about ten. I knew it was wicked, but I had not been able to stop giggling. What if I had handed the narrator a card to replace her description of me? "And here's Sister Pearson in her lovely crystal gown. Sister Pearson's marriage is in big trouble these days because of her husband's homosexuality, and she cries a lot, but she's hanging in there, so let's give her a big hand!"

Then the thought: *What if all the women here had handed in authentic reports of their marriages and we had posted them by the lace and the garters and the pictures? Perhaps then I would not have felt so alone.*

I took off my dress quickly and quickly helped to take down our display. I wanted to get out of the chapel. I felt that I was not breathing right. Even the air was slightly yellowed. I picked up my little candy swan and pictures and headed for the door. I had to go where I could cry if I had to, I had to get out. . . . Out of Utah? Could I possibly work out what lay before me under the eyes of everyone who knew me? The eternal family is such a fundamental concept in Mormonism. I loved my people and my community, but we seemed to judge each other on our marriages, not necessarily their quality, but their survival. Endure to the end, we were always told, and you'll be blessed, in the hereafter if not now.

No one would counsel me just to endure, I knew that. If we did not pull off the miracle, I would surely be encouraged to leave Gerald. And yet I would be judged. To many a divorced woman, for whatever reason, is a failure. Why had I married such a man in the first place, people would wonder. Why hadn't I been able to snap him out of it? Why was I not worthy of the kind of man who could lead me into the celestial kingdom? Our community viewed homosexuality as evil and disgusting. I couldn't bear to have people talking about Gerald as if he were a monster. In all the praying I had done, I had felt strongly that Gerald was as much loved of God as I was. I did not feel that the answer was to banish him or to separate him from his children.

If the worst actually happened and we ended our marriage, could we somehow still maintain a relationship? That would be hard to do here. Crushing judgments and shame would take their toll. When a young man in a nearby town was discovered to be a homosexual, his mother had taken it upon herself to call BYU and have him expelled from school. She then called his place of employment and told them he was gay and should be fired. She called every subsequent place he worked and gave the same information. She told him, "I want you to repent, and I know the only way you'll repent is to be reduced to the gutter. That's what I pray for."

Another Mormon mother discovering that her teenage son had had homosexual encounters did not speak to him for three months or set a place for him at the table. She was arranging to place him in a foster home.

There were better stories. A father who had found his son in a suicide attempt had held him in his arms and wept with him, saying, "You have had to bear this all *alone*. You should not have had to bear it alone. We are with you."

I had also watched a family that I knew quite well. It was fairly open knowledge that their grown son was a homosexual. He was also a wonderful artist, and at each of his exhibits his good solid Mormon family came en masse. They embraced him and exclaimed over his work and let the world know they loved him.

Could I be that brave? Could I stand up in Provo, Utah, and say to everyone, "This is Gerald and I don't understand it either but he is a homosexual. I still love him and I hope you will too."

I was not that brave. If only I were not so well known in Utah. If only Gerald had not borrowed that two thousand dollars and published *Beginnings*. I longed for blessed anonymity, and wished that the drama that was about to begin could be acted out in the safe society of strangers.

We were out in the back eating watermelon after the Fourth of July parade. Nobody in the nation has a better Fourth of July parade than Provo does, and this year's, in honor of the Bicentennial, was especially good. The night before, we had attended a performance of the Tabernacle Choir singing the choral piece, "New Morning Symphony," for which I had written the words. The composer and I had received a standing ovation. Maybe this Independence Day I was feeling unusually brave, unusually independent.

"Gerald," I said, "as long as we're going to move to a different house, maybe we ought to *really* move. Maybe we should leave Utah altogether. Move to California."

Gerald looked at me in amazement. "*You* would leave *Utah?* You really would?"

"I've been thinking about it a lot. I would."

Before we went into the house we laid our plans. I knew that in some ways trading Utah for California was risky, but I also knew that geography was not going to be the final determinant in Gerald's decisions.

It was not easy to do. Just about everyone I loved was in Utah. My roots had been in Utah for four generations. I loved the state and I loved the people, but the ground under me was the ground of a new frontier. On August 17, 1976, we packed the moving van and left.

Chapter 9

Brigham Young did not design Walnut Creek, California. I missed the good straight streets and sidewalks and the easy-to-find addresses. But the palm trees! They made up for the streets. *This is not Utah,* I told myself again and again. *Nobody here knows me. Nobody here cares about my strange marriage*! A great weight fell from my shoulders.

They knew me at Church, however. I had to introduce myself in Sunday School and afterward several people came up and told me how much they'd enjoyed my writing and how glad they were to have me there. Ward members were friendly but not intrusive. I wanted badly to be left alone, and they must have sensed it. Gerald and I met with the bishop, as all new members do, and Gerald explained that because of some personal feelings he himself would not be attending Church. The bishop did not pry, but said Gerald would be welcome at any activities he might care to attend. The next week the bishop called and invited us to go water-skiing with a small group of ward members.

"Come on, you guys, move it along," Gerald said at breakfast one morning soon after we had arrived. "We're going to San Francisco to see the sights. And the ocean!"

We drove toward the Bay Bridge and sang songs and vied to see who would be the first to spot a sailboat.

"Can we get a sailboat when we get rich?" John asked.

"Sure," said Gerald. "Soon as we get rich, we'll buy us a sailboat."

I liked to hear Gerald talk about the future. It was reassuring when he spoke so confidently.

The children were wonderful tourists and Gerald was a wonderful guide, but I kept looking at the men, the young men with short hair and short beards who often walked in pairs. At the Chinese Tea Gardens two young men were holding hands. I was behind the rest of the family with Katy and I hurried her along so she wouldn't see. The small familiar waves of terror moved within me.

We spent the evening at an outdoor concert that featured Beverly Sills. There were lots of families there, lots of old people and some young men, but none who held hands. I felt safer there. The children and Gerald cavorted around on the grass and we ate the supper we had brought. Just before the concert began a woman who was sitting behind us came over and spoke to me. "You have such lovely children," she said. "I've been watching you. You're a beautiful, beautiful family."

Of course we were. We always would be. The woman had seen it. Gerald saw it. We had a wonderful family and it came first. It would always come first. For time and all eternity.

Gerald took a job as cook at a seafood restaurant in San Francisco. His natural talent was quickly recognized as well as his industry and his gift for getting along with people.

"They're opening a second restaurant next year at the Embarcadero Center," Gerald told us at supper one evening. "They said there might be a place for me as manager of the kitchen."

"Great!" I was happy to see something good opening up for Gerald in his work. He had put such energy into the work of other people; it was his turn for a break.

Gerald and I had not directly discussed the pain that lay between us for some time, but we had brought it with us from

Utah just as we had brought the little wooden rocker, the painting of the windmill, and the oak filing cabinet. I kept it boxed up, in the back of the back closet. It was not mentioned until Emily's baptism. She had turned eight before we left Provo and was overdue for the ordinance that makes one officially a member of the Church. Gerald knew that I would insist on the ceremony, but he was dreading it.

"I don't want to turn our children over to an organization that will teach them to hate their father," he said.

"Gerald," I responded quickly, "you know that there is no person or organization anywhere on this earth that could teach your children to hate you. You know they love and adore you, and they always will."

"But the Church will tell them that I am *evil.*"

"Look, Gerald," I said. "I understand your feelings toward the Church, but without it you wouldn't have developed into the person you are, or have the spiritual interests you do. I think the Church has done a lot for you."

There were tears in Gerald's eyes when he answered me. "That's the trouble, Blossom. I love the Church. *And the Church detests me.* That's why it hurts so much!"

My brother David came from Sacramento to baptize Emily. Gerald spent much of the evening in the office he had in the garage. At one point Emily went out to see him and soon I went out to get some more ice cream from the freezer. Gerald was holding Emily on the big cushions. About ten minutes later she came in.

"Daddy was crying," she said to me. "He cried on my cheek. I asked him why and he said we'd talk about it when I get older. Why was Daddy crying?"

"Just because he loves you, Emily," I said.

That first Christmas in our new home Gerald decided he wanted to establish a family tradition that would make

Christmas more meaningful. One evening in the midst of the season's excitement, he turned out all the lights in the house and gave each of us an unlighted candle.

"Now I want you to try to feel the darkness," Gerald said. "See how dark, how really dark everything is. A house without light is like a world without love. This is the way the world was without the love that Jesus brought. He came and brought his love that gave light to everything. Now sit still while I go get something."

Gerald went out of the living room and came back with a large white candle. He set the lighted candle on the table in front of us.

"I want you to think of this light as the light of Christ. It's there for us, but we have to open ourselves to it, take it into ourselves. What are some ways we can get the light into ourselves? Emily, what do you think?"

"Prayer."

"Good. Johnny, how about you?"

"Loving and kissing people."

"Aaron?"

"I dunno. Being good?"

"Sure. Blossom?"

"Reading the things that Jesus did and trying to do them."

"And one thing that brings the light into me," Gerald said, "is meditating. Now I want you each to take the candle that I gave you and light it from the big candle and think about how you're going to have more light in your life."

We each lit our candles. The children were very intent, very quiet. As I watched Gerald help Katy, I was overcome with gratitude for such a good man. *Such* a good man. There was some mistake in that painful thing we had been dealing with. Gerald was not really a homosexual. He was really a beautiful man who taught his children about the light. All my prayers would be answered, all my fasting would be effective, and whatever was troubling Gerald would be lifted.

Two weeks later Gerald told me he was going to a meeting that evening in the city.

"A meeting? Of what?" I asked.

"It's a support group called Gay Fathers."

I had been facing the other way, watering a plant. The water spilled over the sides of the pot, over the little plate and onto the table.

"Don't go, Gerald," I said softly without turning around. "Please don't go."

He came around so he could look at me and sat down at the table in front of me.

"I have got to go, Blossom," he said. "I have got to start facing things. *We* have got to start facing things. I am a homosexual man and I have to figure out what that means and find a life that will let that part of me live."

"But Gerald," I cried, "even if it's hard for you, even if it's a personal sacrifice, don't you think it's worth it? Even if you are gay, maybe you should ignore it, just *make yourself ignore it.* Be celibate altogether if you want to. Catholic priests do it. Lots of people who don't marry for one reason or another do it. Even if it was a mistake, you are deeply involved in a family. You have four children! You have a wife! Even if it was a mistake, we are *here*! Aren't we worth some sacrifice?"

Gerald slowly took his hands from his face and looked at them and then at me. "If I could solve the problem by cutting off these hands, I would do it. This is not just a physical thing. It involves *all* of me—all of my personality, all of my identity, even all of my spirit."

"Gerald, your spirit is not gay!"

"No one's spirit is gay *or* straight, but right now, in this life, as Gerald Pearson, I am a homosexual. I have got to follow that. You're right. I could be celibate. If I didn't *need* to know and feel and experience, if I were content to just live on the surface of things, I could give it all up. I could squash myself down and bind myself up and tell life to go around and not through me. But, Blossom, I'm a person who needs to live! I am not an empty person. I've got to plunge into life and find out what's there for me! If I don't, I'll gradually die, piece by piece by piece. And I'll be of no value to anybody, not you or the children or myself!"

Why did Gerald have that tremendous, restless, driving energy? That same energy that drew me to him in the first place was now taking him away from me! Gerald's expansiveness, his warmth, his appetite for living was what I had always loved about him. But now those things were my enemy! He was like the little wooden Don Quixote he had bought in Europe and loved so much. The male and female bronze, the perfect couple, were there above the television, but Gerald was like the Don Quixote on the other shelf, alone, adventuresome—and mad.

I lay on the bed pretending to read while Gerald got ready to go to the meeting. I could see him through the bathroom door in the same ritual I had observed hundreds of times. Tonight it seemed different. Was he spending more time than usual in front of the mirror trimming his mustache? How dare he put on after-shave lotion? How dare he look so handsome?

" 'Bye, Blossom. See you later."

As he shut the door, I slid from the bed to my knees and poured out to God how much I hated my husband. All his smooth explanations and rationalizations didn't make it right. It was still crazy, still wrong! I would leave as soon as I could. I would take the children far away and leave Gerald to the fate he deserved. It would not work out for him and I would be glad. He would grow old, alone and bitter, and he would finally see what he had given up. And I would be happy at his misery.

I cried for a while, still on my knees, and then was quiet.

It felt good to hate. Hatred was strong and solid, something you could hang on to.

I'd often heard stories of dramatic answers to prayers, of voices, visions, and wonderful revelations. I'd never had any of those. The only voice that ever spoke to me sounded suspiciously like my own, but when it did speak it sounded very much like a wiser, older friend. Now this voice said to me simply, "You don't hate Gerald. There is a better way. Just be patient. Don't let Gerald go until you can let him go with love."

My hatred lifted from me and I even managed to sleep a little before I heard our car in the driveway.

"Oh, Blossom, it is so good to be with people who *understand* me," Gerald said as he climbed into bed. "There were about thirty guys there. Most of the men are divorced, but several are still married. Ron and his wife—I talked to him a lot after—he and his wife are working things out just fine. They have a strong commitment to each other, but each lets the other have whatever other relationships they need."

"You mean I could have other relationships?"

Gerald thought only for a moment. "If you needed them, yes. If they were important to you."

Receiving such quick permission to be unfaithful filled me with rage. "But I don't need them. What I need is to have a *monogamous, committed relationship*. Why isn't that need as valid as yours?"

"It is, Blossom," Gerald said quietly. "Of course it is. But I wish you would try."

"I have been trying."

"I wish you would meet Ron and his wife."

"No, I can't."

"Then we're stuck, aren't we?"

A little moonlight streamed in the window and fell across the bed. Neither of us spoke. The word "divorce" had never been said in any of our conversations. Sometimes we had said, "If worse comes to worst," or "if we can't make things work," but no one had ever said that awful, dark, final word "divorce." But the word hung in the air now, filled the room and pressed itself between us.

"Let's talk tomorrow. Good night, Blossom."

"Good night."

I fasted the next Sunday. And the next. And the next. Often Gerald fasted with me. Neither of us felt that divorce was the answer, at least not yet. The voice in my prayers continued to tell me to be patient, not to give in to hate, to look for a better way. Again I avoided mirrors. Perhaps I could cut my hair so short that I could keep it combed without ever having to look at myself. And why put on lipstick? Why trouble with eyeliner and mascara? Those were things to make you look more feminine. Why want to look more feminine? Why would *anyone* want to look feminine?

Again the masculine world bore down on me with crushing force. Male *was* better. God was still male, wasn't he? His face, at least symbolically, wore a beard. The Church still preferred men, didn't it? In the chart used in Sunday School class a few weeks ago, the arrows of authority were vertical and firm: God—man—woman. Maleness is closer to God than femaleness is.

And my husband still—oh, still, still and always—preferred men too.

I led the singing at Primary, the weekly meeting for children. A half hour of cheerfulness once a week exhausted me. I read to my children at bedtime instead of making up "Pegora" stories for them. I put on records instead of singing lullabies, and playing my guitar. I did not want to touch Gerald. And I wrote.

I dim,
I dim—

I have no doubt
If someone blew
I would go out.

I was not the only one who was suffering. Often, I would look at Gerald holding one of the children close, his face a study in pain. Once Gerald caught me crying and pulled me to him.

"Oh, Blossom," he said, "do you know how I feel to see you like this? I love you so much, and I am the *cause* of your *pain*. I hate myself for it! What can I do? What can I do?"

We clung to each other as if we were in a shipwreck. I did not look on Gerald as the clear villain in our drama. It seemed to me now that Gerald's homosexuality was like a force, apart from both of us, that we each had to find a way to deal with.

"I don't want to lose you," said Gerald. "Do you know what my greatest fear is? The greatest fear of all my life? That I will lose you and lose the children, that finally we will not even be friends. That tortures me."

I didn't reply. I could make no promises.

Gerald's work became the focus of most of his energy. The management invited him to become a junior partner for the new restaurant.

"I could own stock in the company," he said, "and if things go well, it'll be worth a lot. Only I'd have to come up with fifteen thousand dollars to invest in order to qualify. I'm not sure I could borrow that."

I thought for a moment. I wanted Gerald to have that opportunity. In spite of our incredible dilemma, I found that I wanted him to succeed. He *deserved* to succeed. Gerald had given his all to building me, building my career and my confidence. It was only fair that he have his chance.

"I think we can do it, Gerald," I said. "It's a great opportunity for you."

"But how?"

"The tour of *My Turn on Earth* is bringing me quite a bit of money right now. I think in the next couple of months we could put that much together."

Gerald looked at me and smiled. "When I get rich, Blossom—and I'm going to—I'm going to set you up for the rest of your life. I've already got a long list of things I'm going to do for you."

We scraped together twelve thousand, and my stepmother, Gladys, loaned us the final three. Gerald became a junior partner in the new restaurant.

"We'll be working day and night to prepare for the opening," he explained to us, "so you guys won't be seeing a whole lot of me for the next few months. Sometimes we'll be working until midnight, and I'm going to take a room in San Francisco so I won't have to travel so much. But I'll be out here on the weekends and also on Wednesday night."

A room in San Francisco. I heard a small, muffled sound in my mind, like the quiet closing of a door.

I had been suggesting to Gerald that we find a good counselor to help us make sure we had looked realistically at all our alternatives and were prepared to make a final decision about our marriage. He was very willing, but asked that we put it off until after the opening of the restaurant. Final decisions would be very painful for him and he didn't want to face that at the same time he had to face enormous pressures at work. I agreed. I wasn't quite ready to let go either.

One evening the telephone rang.

"Sister Pearson? This is the stake Relief Society president in San Rafael. We're having a conference in May and we would love to have you be our speaker. We just learned you were in the area and are so thrilled!"

Another speaking invitation. I had developed a standard reply. "Oh, I wish I could. But for family reasons I'm not doing any speaking now."

The following evening the phone rang again. "Sister Pearson? I spoke to you last night about coming to San Rafael. My counselors and I just could not accept the fact that you're not speaking anymore. We've been fasting and praying about it since I spoke to you last night. And . . . I know this is a strange, maybe an impertinent thing to ask of you, but . . . our women need so badly to hear what you have to say. We feel that nobody could inspire them like you could. So we decided to ask you to please pray about this. If you still don't feel you can come, we'll accept that."

I hung up the telephone and sank down into a chair, shaking with anger. How dare they? How dare they fast and pray about me? I am *none of their business.* I wanted to get away from all that. I wanted just to be left alone. I am empty! I have nothing to give! I have no answers for myself, let alone for anybody else . . .

"Heavenly Father, I do not want to go out speaking again. I do not want to go out and pretend. . . ." Pretend? That was my own voice talking back to me. Pretend what? Do you think you're the only person who smiles when she doesn't feel like it? Are you the only one who has met a catastrophe? Of the five hundred women who will be in San Rafael, how many do you think never cry? Maybe they don't need to hear from the rare and perfect woman who has got it all together. Maybe they need to hear from someone who is struggling just like they are, someone who hurts a lot but has not given up yet, someone who is trying desperately to find a Christ-like answer to a horrendous problem. Maybe they need to hear from *you.* And maybe it wouldn't do you any harm either.

I sat on the stand in San Rafael watching the five hundred women fill the chapel, and a warmth filled my heart.

I loved Mormon women. They were not God's only true women, I knew that, but they were *my* women. No women anywhere tried harder to do what they felt was right. Many of them were a little more docile and unquestioning than I'd wish, and I wanted to inject them with some of the fire of Emmeline B. Wells. But not today. Today we would talk about growth, pain, and love, because I needed to talk about it, and because out of five hundred women surely there was one who had a handicapped child or an alcoholic husband or a son stealing money for drugs or a husband who walked out on her last week. Surely there was a woman who had already taken the pills she felt she needed to get through the day. But they were *here*. They were involved in this mutual effort to lift. They had not given up.

I spoke, and the act of speaking made me believe. Pain is a necessary element in growth, I said, and love is the final standard. Like the pioneers whose crops were being destroyed by the crickets, and who were saved by the sea gulls that miraculously appeared, we can each ask for and receive some small miracle designed to our unique devastation:

> It's time, Father,
> For the gulls, I think.
> My arms shake
> From flailing my field.
> I sink,
> Broken as the little stalks
> Beneath their devouring burden.
>
> I yield it all to you.
> Who alone can touch all things.
> It's time, Father,
> For the gulls.
>
> I will be still,
> And listen for their wings.

One day Gerald rushed into the house with a bouquet of baby carnations he had bought in the city. And then from behind his back he produced a book.

"Ta dum! Look at that, Blossom. I knew when I saw this, you had to have it."

I reached for the book and read the title. *When God Was a Woman.* Was I smiling at Gerald's enthusiasm or at the marvelous, shocking title? I stayed up late for several nights. The book was too good to be true. For thousands of years the human family saw our Creator as *Mother?* The idea was universal and *respectable?* I had heard of goddess worship, but never Goddess worship with a capital G. It was never to be taken seriously. It was an evidence of corruption. I had wanted so passionately for heaven to validate my femaleness. But heaven was so . . . masculine! Could I have been wrong? Perhaps whatever our Creator finally is, the feminine is there as fully as the masculine. The poor, wounded female in me opened her eyes in amazement.

I went to bookstores and libraries. I got up early and stayed up late reading everything I could find from historians and mythologists. I felt the same half joy, half rage as when Aunt Mamie had given me those first issues of *Women's Exponent* in Dingle, Idaho. *Why was I never told this?* I had hungered all my life for the Motherless house we live in to be filled with the female as well as the male. Only now did I learn that the word "Elohim," in its original meaning, embraces the feminine as much as it does the masculine and that in the earliest recorded creation story, the earth is formed by the Mother of the Gods and that the Christian Gnostics spoke of the Father, the Mother, and the Son.

All these accounts, of course, made no difference finally. God was whatever God chose to be no matter what the ancients thought or what the historians and mythologists wrote. But the books gave me enough courage to look into my own heart. And what I read there changed my life. Of course heaven is not a masculine institution! Of course our Creator is male and female in some absolute, final, wonderful balance! Of course my woman's hands and woman's breasts reflect the divine as entirely as the body of a man!

I had always had that small hope to go on, that one statement by the Prophet Joseph Smith, radical in its day, that we have a Heavenly Mother as well as a Heavenly Father. But no one ever talked about it. It was one of the mysteries. A couple of times a year we would sing in Church about the dual deity in the words of Eliza R. Snow:

> In the heavens are parents single?
> No, the thought makes reason stare:
> Truth is reason, truth eternal
> Tells me I've a mother there.
>
> When I leave this frail existence—
> When I lay this mortal by;
> Father, Mother, may I meet you
> In your royal court on high?

I had sung those words and had been filled with longing to make them mean something in my life. But I had never dared to truly make room for the Divine Couple. Oh, but I needed the Divine Couple now. The wound to the woman in me could only be healed with the help of the Woman in Heaven.

Cautiously I unbound the old ropes from my imagination and gave it permission to move. I had had no heavenly vision and I expected none. I invited the Divine Couple into my mind and they came. He did not have a beard. She did not follow three feet behind. They came together and moved together and danced together in a perfect pas de deux. Out of their absolute unity sprang suns and moons and stars. Light flashed from their touch and the sparks were all of us. Mountains rose and hummingbirds flew where they stepped, mementoes of their mutual strength and gentleness.

I seemed now to trust God more. I had been wrong.

God did not prefer men. In the heavens, I now believed with all my heart, femaleness was as operative and as magnificent and as desirable as maleness. Perhaps I was not, might never be, half of a couple where balance worked. But in the eternal, in the archetypal, there was that Divine Couple, and for now that would do. I would let them hold me and heal me.

Almost, almost I was ready to let Gerald go with love.

Then I had the dream. It came, I know, from a higher consciousness that uses symbols in dreams to work out the drama of our lives. In the dream I was on a warm and beautiful island with a man. We were a *couple,* as fully as anyone has ever been. I woke up with a feeling of complete delight and well being. I felt healed, desired, loved. The feeling would not leave me. I wore it all day, as tangible as a sweater and as warm. The man in the dream was someone I had gone out with for several years before we both married other people. I hadn't seen Fred in years, but dreaming of him was like the birthday party that awful September that reminded me I was a person before I ever knew Gerald. I was using this dream to remind myself that there *was* a time when I did not feel ugly and rejected, when a man looked at me the way a woman wants to be looked at. I had forgotten! Until the dream I had forgotten what it felt like to be desired.

I got out an old tape recording that Fred and I had made in college when we used to read play scenes together. "From *The Rainmaker,*" my voice said. I listened to Fred's wonderful voice and Starbuck's wonderful words:

> "Believe in yourself, Lizzie."
> "I've got nothing to believe in."
> "You're a woman. Believe in that."
> "How can I when nobody else will?"
> "You've got to believe it first."

Day after day I sat alone in my room and listened to the tape and let it nourish me and heal me. "You're a woman. Believe in that." Eventually, I began to see something different in the mirror. I looked—not quite beautiful—but it was true that I had wonderful eyes.

One evening Gerald was sitting on the piano bench with Emily, and I was listening to them sing. It had been a long time since I had been able to touch Gerald. I had had nothing to give him. But now, listening to them, I felt strangely full. I walked across the room and stood behind Gerald. I put my hands on his shoulders and began to move the palms along the muscles of Gerald's back and shoulders. Then I leaned over and kissed the back of his neck. He took my fingers and held them to his lips for a long moment. A wet drop ran down the back of my hand.

Chapter 10

Gerald wanted to go dining and dancing to celebrate our twelfth and what we both knew would be our last wedding anniversary together. Though he preferred disco, he chose a place that played the old-time dance music that I loved. I didn't really want to go, but he was doing it for me and so I did it for him. It was a strange, but fitting ritual.

At dinner Gerald pulled out two envelopes. "An early birthday present," he said, handing me one. In it was an airplane ticket to Carmel and back and a letter saying, "Congratulations! You are the lucky recipient of four peaceful days all to yourself in beautiful Carmel. You will spend three expense-paid nights at the charming Pine Inn on Ocean Avenue, just a stone's throw from the beach. While there you may read, sleep, eat, think, not think, do anything you wish. Happy Birthday, Sweetheart. Thanks again for being born and sharing your life with me. Love, Gerald."

I looked up and smiled. "Thanks, kid. Can you afford this? You're not rich yet."

"Sure, I can. I wish it were more." Then from the other envelope he pulled out a piece of paper. "A poem for you. 'To my dearest Blossom, in answer to your question: "How do you suppose it is that we chose to live this life together?"'"

In the poem Gerald explored his belief in reincarnation

and karma, that the same people meet one another in life after life until they finally learn the lessons of love that they came to learn. The poem expressed his continuing love for me. I listened to him read, so earnest, so open. Of course Gerald loved me. I had always known that. He loved me as a person with all his heart. And he loved me as a woman as best he could.

"Next life, Blossom," Gerald said as he put the poem back in its envelope and handed it to me, "let's you and me ask for something really simple. Let's be peasants together in Scotland and have nothing complicated to work out and just enjoy each other. Would you try it again with me some-time, Blossom?"

"Sure, Gerald. But what if we only get one? What if the Mormons are right and this is all we get?"

"Then will you come down and visit me? And bring a picnic? At least they ought to let us have a picnic together."

I smiled. "I'll bring a picnic."

The restaurant had finally opened and was a wonderful success, and Gerald felt he now had the emotional energy to face whatever steps we needed to take. He would not agree to see a Mormon counselor, so I called a nationally known sex therapist in San Francisco. Although he was now retired from counseling, he said our case interested him.

"There are few absolute heterosexuals and few absolute homosexuals," he told us. "We all exist on something like this scale from zero to six, depending on how much sexual response we feel toward someone of our own sex. Carol Lynn is a zero. Gerald, from what he is telling me here, would probably be about a four. That is not going to change. I have followed the histories of thousands of homosexual men. I have never seen a case in which one in the higher numbers—four, five, or six—has changed to a zero or a one or a two. I think it is possible for one on the homosexual end of the scales to *add to* their homosexual orientation the possibility of relating sexually to a woman. Gerald has already done that. But I have never seen the primary homosexual need *replaced* with a heterosexual need. One can, of course, stifle the need altogether. Some people do, but for most healthy human beings that's asking a lot."

We met with the therapist individually and then together again, discussing with him when and how much to tell the children. When we left his office after the fourth visit, our future was firm.

On Thanksgiving evening, after dinner was over and the kitchen was clean and games had been played and the children were in bed, Gerald and I sat in the family room beside the fire and planned our divorce. We drank peppermint tea and even managed to laugh a few times. We would do the divorce ourselves. No attorneys were needed. I would get the house and have custody of the children. Gerald could spend as much time with us as he wanted. He could even leave some clothes in my closet. He could take the children into the city, but they were to see nothing there that they were not accustomed to seeing here. He would answer any questions the children asked, but he would not tell them he was homosexual until quite a way down the road. I felt strongly they should not have to deal with that now.

I drove Gerald down to BART, the train station, and we sat in my yellow Volvo station wagon waiting for the midnight train. I put my hand on his knee and he covered it with his own.

"Gerald," I said, "we're still sealed, you know. Whether it's by the Mormon priesthood or by karma or by twelve years of taking care of each other and having four children together, we will always be sealed. You're on a path I can't travel as your wife, but I can travel it as your friend. I will always be your friend."

"Thank you, Blossom." The train was coming and Gerald leaned over and gave me a kiss. "Good night, sweetheart," he said and opened the door.

I watched the lights of the train grow smaller in the distance and disappear. My cheeks were wet, but that was nothing new. That was usual.

There he went, Don Quixote on his mad quest, dreaming his impossible dream, a bright knight plunging into the unknown. "Good night, sweetheart," he says as he leaves his wife in search of his lover, his companion, and his soul mate. It was mad. He was not afraid, but I was afraid for him, no longer angry but now sister, wife, mother, worrying and praying while the brother, husband, son goes out to battle.

I did not trust San Francisco. I did not trust Castro Street. I knew that every man there was just somebody's son, somebody's brother, even somebody's husband, and certainly a child of God. But who out there would care about Gerald as I did? Who would appreciate that wonderful, strangely naive brightness? Who would appreciate his spiritual hungers? Would Gerald be eaten alive out there? Was I throwing him to the wolves? I gave Gerald back to God and threw a blessing around him like a cloak, like the white light that meditators wear for protection.

The next weekend we told the children. We decided to do it before Christmas so we could use the holidays to cushion the blow with an especially happy time. I sat everyone down in the family room with two plates of chocolate chip cookies, and for the first time in my life I did not ration them out.

Emily sat on Gerald's lap. It was not that he loved her

more. It was just that he had loved her longer, for ten years. There was a bond between them that was very strong. John and Aaron, now seven and eight, lay on the floor, flipping cookie crumbs at each other. Katy, who was only three years old, was upstairs napping.

I concentrated on my breathing for a minute or two and then began. "Well, you guys," I said. "We need to have a talk about something really important. You'll be glad to know that Gerald's work schedule is easing off somewhat and he'll be able to come out and spend more time with us. But he's going to keep his apartment in the city. We are still a family. We will always be a family, but there is a change coming up that you children need to know about. Gerald and I have decided that we can help each other better and be happier as best friends instead of as husband and wife." There. I had said it. I had said it and I was still breathing. "Does that sound okay to you?"

The children looked at me without speaking. Finally John said, "Well, yeah. I guess so."

"You mean," said Emily, "like . . . like a divorce?"

"Like a divorce," said Gerald. Then he hugged Emily. "Life is full of surprises, isn't it, Em?"

Emily looked at me in amazement. "Why? You don't fight. I've never seen you fight one time!"

"Blossom and I have different needs, Em. Someday you'll understand that."

Emily turned and buried her face in Gerald's chest.

"I know this is a surprise," said Gerald, "but I want you to understand what it does *not* mean. It does not mean that I will no longer be your father. I'll be out here a lot and we'll do a lot together. And it does not mean that Carol Lynn and I no longer love each other. In fact, we feel better toward each other now than we have for some time. Aaron, what are you feeling right now?"

"I dunno. Guess I'll get used to it." Aaron was a tough man, a builder. He'd be able to hammer this into some kind of shape that he could deal with.

"John?"

"Well, if we're going to still see you a lot, why should I sit in the corner and cry?" Whatever disappointment came along John always found a way to look on the bright side.

"Emily, how about you? Can you manage this?"

Emily shrugged her shoulders, unwilling to trust her voice.

Gerald squeezed and tickled her a little until a half smile came.

"Sure, you will. You'll be fine. You'll all be fine. And so will Blossom. And so will I."

"For right now this is our private family business," I added. "You're not to tell anyone."

"Not even at show-and-tell?" asked John.

"No, John. Not even at show-and-tell."

We talked more and then hurried the children out to get their sweaters so we wouldn't be late for *The Wiz*. As they left, Gerald and I embraced in relief at a hard thing finally done. Aaron came back in to see us and said, "Me too." He put his arms around our legs and hugged, and I knew he was going to be all right.

Gerald had decided that he would tell his parents about the divorce and about his homosexuality at the same time. He was understandably apprehensive. So many gay men he knew had been met with rejection and horror when they brought the news. I had to be in Utah for a speaking engagement and I suggested that Gerald come at the same time so I could see his parents afterward and let them know that I was okay and that I still loved them all. I called him at their home after the encounter to find out how it went.

"Oh, Blossom," he said emotionally, "it was wonderful. I'm so angry that I didn't do it a long time ago. I've missed so many good years with them through fear. We sat down and I told them everything. No one spoke for a couple of minutes. Finally I said, 'Well, say something. Say *something*. Yell at me—hit me—throw me out if you want to.' My sister was the first one to speak. She said, *'Jerry*, you don't know your parents very well, do you? They don't throw their kids out.' And she went on to tell me that when she had a problem—a pretty big problem—and didn't know how they would respond, they just helped and loved her through it. And then Mom said, 'Jerry, I won't pretend that I really understand what you've just told me. I don't understand it, but you are still our son. We love you. We will always love you.' And even my dad"—Gerald's voice broke—"even my dad, knowing all this, he still *hugged me*! Oh, Blossom, I should have done this a long time ago."

My own family and friends took the news well. It was startling to them, of course. Divorce is not supposed to happen. Homosexuality is not supposed to happen. But when dogma collides with experience, when the people involved are those you love, you see with different eyes. Without exception, the people in my life gave only love and support. And they gave the same to Gerald, even though they were baffled.

Gerald threw himself with great enthusiasm into his quest. His long-term goal was to find the man with whom he could share his life. And his short-term goal was to be a part of a cause that would at once raise the spiritual consciousness of the gay world and cultivate tolerance and understanding in the straight world.

By this time I also had learned about the history of the gay movement. I knew about the Stonewall riot of 1969 when New York police had entered a gay bar on Christopher Street in a raid that was one of many, routine and arbitrary. Usually the raids ended in several arrests and various injuries, but this time, to the surprise of everyone, the homosexuals refused to take their punishment passively. A brawl ensued. The "sissies" were fighting back. Word spread and the gay community turned out in force. Cars were overturned, fires were lit, and police were sent to the hospital. When the riot was over, a new chapter had begun. Homosexual people across the nation began to look at themselves differently.

I had never found it hard to sympathize with the underdog. I certainly sympathized with my Mormon ancestors when they were beaten and burned out of their houses and given an "extermination" order by the governor because of their unusual beliefs and practices. And I understood Brigham Young finally saying, "No! No more!" in Utah when it appeared that a U.S. Army was on its way with further terror. They prepared to meet the enemy, drove off the Army's horses, stampeded their cattle, and burned their supply trains. I could understand that. Mormons deserved rights.

I certainly sympathized with Susan B. Anthony daring to cast her vote even though it meant jail. Women deserved rights. I sympathized with Martin Luther King marching in the face of threats and bullets. Blacks deserved rights. And I could understand a homosexual person finally saying, "No more beatings!"

And yet, it was so strange, this gay Utopia that was being built just over the bridge. Having released Gerald, I no longer looked on San Francisco as the enemy. My own pain had been lifted. My love for Gerald had changed from that of wife to that of sister. Still—I continued to have reservations as I studied the phenomenon. When I discussed my doubts with Gerald, he said, "Give us a little time, Blossom. There may be a lot that's crazy in the gay life, but this is a brand-new culture. We haven't learned from our mistakes yet. Guys come here who have been made to feel like dirt all their lives. Suddenly, what they've had to steal before, in the dark when no one's looking, is all around them, free for the taking. Of course they go crazy! They run around like a little kid in a candy store!"

A candy store? Suddenly I remembered that awful dream I had the first year we were married, when Gerald was grabbing all the cookies he could carry, though they cost a dollar each. He wouldn't listen to my screams for him to stop. Now I was frightened again, and wanted to cry out to him, but I knew that again I would not be heard.

Earlier that year I had been asked by the Utah State Department of Education to write a film on sexual responsibility. I had begun it with a powerful statement from Will and Ariel Durant, historians who had studied the human condition all their lives. If a person is "unchecked by custom, morals, or laws," they had written, "he may ruin his life before he . . . understands that sex is a river of fire that must be banked and cooled by a hundred restraints if it is not to consume in chaos both the individual and the group."

That statement seemed *so reasonable* to me. Why couldn't they see it? Why couldn't all the marchers in the annual Gay Pride parade see it? I was with them all the way in their demand for civil rights and in their demand to be viewed as valuable human beings. But I was not with them in their insistence on a life that had no real sexual restraints. They were riding a river of fire and they wanted Gerald to ride with them. I was afraid.

About the time we decided on the divorce, Gerald learned that a group was forming called the San Francisco Gay Men's Chorus. He immediately joined.

"This is the kind of thing we need to be doing, Blossom," he said. "To show the world and each other that gay men are not just queers who swish around or wear chains to S and M bars. We're lawyers and accountants and artists. We're singers!

The chorus is doing our first concert just before Christmas. Will you come?"

Could I bear to see Gerald in his new life? I did not want to go, but I could tell how much it meant to him.

"Sure, Gerald. I'll come."

On December 10, 1978, I took the train into the city and then, according to Gerald's careful instructions, a streetcar. I walked up the steps of the school as one might walk up the steps of a hospital for necessary surgery. A large, enthusiastic crowd was entering, most of them young men, but many who were older—men, couples, women. I was early, but already the hall was filling fast. There was an electricity in the air, an anticipation that something unusual was about to happen. I found a seat toward the front beside an older woman.

I practiced my breathing for a few moments, read the program, and then studied the woman beside me. Her presence here must be a whole story, I thought to myself, just like mine is.

"Do you have someone singing tonight?" I asked, smiling at her.

"Yes," she said. "My son. And you?"

I paused for only a moment. "My husband," I said.

She turned away with a sigh and we did not speak further.

The lights dimmed and the Gay Freedom Marching Band began the program. I found myself relaxing a little. It was just music. Just good instrumental music, played by good musicians. The band marched off to tremendous applause.

And then I heard the voices. From the back of the hall I heard the voices and something caved inside my chest and made me press my hands against it hard. I turned, as did everyone in the audience. Marching down both aisles, the chorus entered. Over one hundred handsome young men wearing white shirts and dark pants and red carnations. They were smiling with all that was in them and singing "If My Friends Could See Me Now." They smiled and sang their way onto the stage and I pressed my hands to my chest harder.

The mantle of comfort I had worn for months was suddenly gone. Perhaps if I pressed very hard, I could keep from pouring out. There, near the center, was Gerald, smiling, with all his good light shining. Gerald in white. I had seen him in white before. In the temple in white. In the delivery room in white. And now in white in the San Francisco Gay Men's Chorus.

They sang well, but I did not hear the music. I was pulled through it into the experience. They sang "O Come, O Come, Emmanuel," just like anybody else might sing a beautiful Christmas song. And "Once in Royal David's City." They sang serious pieces and light pieces. I could almost laugh with the rest of the audience at the humorous overtones in "My Buddy." But I could not laugh, I could not, at the series of three old English love songs, the first telling of courting a maid, and the third expressing the realization that it cannot be. "I thank you for all of the joys we did share," they sang. "And know that your love will do better elsewhere."

The concert concluded on a tremendous high. The audience went wild. I found Gerald afterward and made my way to him through the crowd that was hugging and laughing. He threw his arms around me.

"How was it, Blossom?"

"Sounded great. It was a beautiful concert."

"Hey, is this your wife, Gerald?" A tall, beaming man interrupted us.

"Sure is. Blossom, this is Tom. Tom, Carol Lynn."

Tom pumped my arm enthusiastically. "I'm from Utah too! I was telling Gerald the only mistake I made in my divorce was that I got the *Journal of Discourses* and Sheryl got all the Carol Lynn Pearson books. I am *so* glad to meet you. Gerald talks about you all the time. Great night, huh? See you."

Tom hugged me and moved on.

Gerald walked me out to the streetcar. As we made our way through the hugging, laughing, smiling crowd, Gerald said, "Tom was a bishop just last year. There's a whole group of us in the chorus. We're sort of the Tabernacle Choir section."

It was good to be out in the coolness of the night.

"How's your heart, Blossom?" Gerald had taken to asking me that often, wanting to know what was really happening under what seemed to be a good adjustment. There was not a lot he could do for me, but it helped to know that he cared.

"I'll be all right. Tonight was hard."

"For me too. I found when I came out that I was looking for your face. Thanks for coming. It meant a lot to me. You'll be okay? Should I ride with you to BART?"

"No. I'll be fine."

"Good night, sweetheart."

Chapter 11

Four children feels like twice that many when the number of parents is cut in half. During the time that Gerald was discovering his new life in San Francisco, I was discovering what single parenthood was all about. Gerald had in mind that he would spend Wednesday evenings and all day Saturday with us, but I knew the Wednesday evenings would soon disappear. Essentially I was on my own. The emotional, physical, transportational, and most of the financial needs of four children fell on me. Millions of women did it. My pioneer foremothers had done it often, when their husbands died of typhoid or were sent away on missions for years at a time. My husband was away on his own strange mission and I was alone doing the best I could. The day I took the boys fishing at the Lafayette reservoir and John's line got all tangled up in the reel, I was dramatically insufficient. After fifteen or twenty minutes of trying to fix it, I threw the pole down with a "Damn!"

The boys looked at me in amazement. They had never heard such language from their mother. I sent them off to find a park official to help them, while I continued to swear. Damn it anyway! Why did *I* have to deal with fishing poles? Why did I have to carry the whole weight while Gerald went off to seek his fortune? I sat on the bank of the reservoir and threw rocks into the water and cried tears of frustration. Doing it alone was just *too hard*.

Still I knew that Gerald had not totally abandoned us. He suffered from knowing there were responsibilities he had abdicated. The night John slammed his finger in the car door and called Gerald up for some comfort, Gerald said to me, "I can't tell you how awful I feel. I should be there. I should *be* there." But he was not there. Irrevocable decisions had been made and he was not there.

At the same time, I must say that in another way he was *always* there. The time that he spent with them was always meaningful and nourishing to the children. Often he brought out music to play for them, or something to read to them, such as a newspaper article telling of an Indian swami bearing purple chrysanthemums who had flown his motorized kite over the Berlin Wall to East Germany "to prove that love and flowers can overcome barriers better than bombs."

His birthday and Christmas gifts to the children were selected with much thought and love. He always sat down with them to plan Mother's Day and my birthday, making sure that gifts were bought and breakfast in bed was served. And every possible special family day was celebrated with one of Gerald's incomparable feasts. Strange though our life was, I knew that my children had more of their father than many children whose fathers came home from work every day. When Gerald gave me a beautifully framed picture of his aura—the pad of his thumb taken with Kirlian photography and looking like a rising sun—I knew it was symbolic. He wanted at least that to be with us always, to remind us of his light.

As I went through my days as a single parent, I began to notice that along with the exhaustion and the frustration and resentment, there was some growth going on. I had to do things. I was forced into more complete, more intimate contact with the children. There was no way I could generate the kind of easy fun that Gerald did so naturally. But the things that were mine to give, I found myself giving more completely. I could give them the theater. I took them to play auditions and hauled them back and forth to their rehearsals. I took them to piano, guitar, dancing lessons.

I wanted them to feel that we were still a strong family, so—for them as well as for others—I found people who were less strong and brought them home to be nurtured. Battered Women's Alternatives needed "safe home" providers, and we sheltered for two or three days at a time abused women and their children. Our friend Bob had been mugged and needed a place to be taken care of when he got out of the hospital. A young woman had written to me in suicidal despair, and I invited her to come from Utah and spend the summer. We brought two old women from the rest home out to dinner and to see the children in *A Christmas Carol* at the local theater. I *would not* have the children feel sorry for themselves. I would not have them feel that ours was a "broken home." Ours was a strong home. The children were strong people. They found they had a great deal to give and they learned how to give it.

If my children had not reduced me to laughter more often than they reduced me to tears, I could never have made it alone. But each one of them was a smart aleck, a bright and happy person who kept one another and their mother buoyant.

On a day when I had not laughed once, or smiled once, and was exhausted from the inside out, I fixed myself a bubble bath, lit a candle, burned some incense, put on a tape of harp music and climbed into the tub for a few minutes of sensuous indulgence. In a few minutes Emily ran into my bedroom to answer the phone. On her way out she stopped at my bathroom door.

"Mom? What are you *doing* in there?"

"Taking a bath."

"But I smell incense. And I hear music." She lowered her voice dramatically. "Mom, are you *alone?*"

A little while later Emily came back in and tapped on the bathroom door.

"Mom? Good night. Love you."

"Love you too, Emily. Good night."

After a pause, she added, "Good night, Mister."

Whether or not the divorce would affect my career in the Church was something I did not know. As the word got out, would those who had bought my books consider me a fallen woman? Would the Utah publisher to whom we had turned over my books still want me? Would people conclude that a woman like me who speaks in behalf of women's rights and a career just can't keep a marriage together—and let this be an example to us all? I do not know what was said; I only know what was said to me. As the people in my ward became aware of my divorce, and as the people who knew me only from my writing received the information, I met with only helpfulness and kindness. Nobody pried. Nobody judged. I sensed no lessening of respect. I continued to teach the Social Relations lesson in Relief Society, a job that I loved. I continued to receive invitations to speak to Church groups. I continued to have an excellent relationship with my publisher. Here I was in a position I had been warned against all my life. I was a divorced woman and nobody threw stones. Nobody!

Gradually I found a new energy. I took out the little verse I had written in my darkest time and added three new words:

I dim,
I dim—
I have no doubt

If someone blew
I would go out.

I did not.
I must be brighter
Than I thought.

My capacities surprised even my children. Emily had worn me down with begging to have her ears pierced, and when we got to the shop I suddenly decided to have it done myself.

Emily's mouth felt open in amazement. "Mom, what has *happened* to you? In one year you're getting a divorce and having your *ears pierced!*"

When I learned how many of the men I had been friends with in college were gay, I was astonished. I discovered that two women acquaintances were homosexual and eight long-standing male friends were also gay. Eventually I spoke to all these men. Two had married, had children, and divorced. One had been married briefly and then had the marriage annulled. One was in a committed gay relationship that had lasted fifteen years. Two had had various gay relationships and were still hoping for true love. One had been deeply involved in the gay lifestyle, found it was taking him nowhere, had made the decision to be celibate and said that he was very happy. Another had spent years pursuing a gay life and then surprised everyone by marrying and having children; he had counted the cost and decided that more than anything, even if it was not always comfortable, he wanted a family. My life would be less without these good friends, and I shake my head with the irony of it all: I had thought that Gerald was the only homosexual man I had ever known. As the wife of a homosexual man, I had felt so alone. And so, I suppose, had the three wives of my friends—the women who had been left in the wreckage by men who only wanted to do the right thing. Why had we all been so alone?

As to Gerald, the San Francisco Gay Men's Chorus became his home. His enthusiasm, creativity, efficiency, and ability to create good will were recognized, and he soon became a leader in the group. Two years after the chorus was formed, a national tour was planned and Gerald became co-chairman. He gave his all to fund-raising and scheduling the best halls they could get in the biggest cities. Because of differences with the management of the restaurant, Gerald had sold his junior partnership and was living off the money while he gave the better part of a year to the work of the chorus.

Though I was carrying more of the financial burden than was fair, I never judged Gerald on the same scale I might have judged someone else. He had helped me achieve my dream. I released him and blessed him to follow his own. I never wanted to feel responsible for blocking that dream, strange though it was to me. And I knew that his intent was to become financially capable and do wonderful things for his family.

"We got the Kennedy Center in Washington!" he exclaimed one night on the telephone. "So now, besides San Francisco, we're going to Dallas, Minneapolis, Detroit, New York, Washington, D.C., Lincoln, Boston, and Seattle!"

Preparing for the tour was all Gerald could talk about for months. It was his mission, his hope, and his gift to the world. On one of his visits I could tell that Gerald had something on his mind.

"Blossom," he said when we were alone, "I want to take the older children to the concert."

"No."

"At least Emily," he went on. "I don't think it's fair that I can't share this with my children."

"But it would not be sharing just the concert with them. It would be sharing with them everything, the whole story. I don't think they're ready for that. And I know I'm not ready."

We argued. It was the first argument we had had since the separation and Gerald left angry. He did not call for days, but when next we did speak we both apologized. Gerald conceded my authority in this matter, and also that I was doing everything in my power to make things good for him. We were friends again.

In June 1981, the chorus set out on their national tour. They left with a proclamation by San Francisco mayor Dianne Feinstein calling for public recognition and support of this remarkable event.

I knew that Gerald was having the time of his life. He had left in tears of excitement and I knew he would return the same way. Nothing like this had ever happened before. Never had an openly homosexual group of people presented themselves to the world in such a disarming way. It would build bridges, Gerald was certain. It would help destroy prejudice. And I knew that some of Gerald's dreams were being fulfilled as I followed the progress of the tour through the *San Francisco Chronicle*.

Of course, the expected hostilities arose. There were several bomb threats that delayed performances. Twice the teamsters refused to deliver the programs. But the reviews were glowing, opinions were changing, and families were being reunited. After the tour, fourteen gay men's choruses were formed across the country. This is what Gerald had in mind. This is where all his resources had gone: physical, emotional, and financial. He had poured his whole life into the tour and had nearly broken his health over it, but he was seeing a dream come true. Gerald was soaring.

Another part of Gerald's dream, a more personal part, was unfolding at the same time and bringing highs and lows. When Gerald first mentioned a particular friend of his in the city, I searched myself for jealousy and incredibly I found none. I had so succeeded in releasing Gerald that I could look on his quest as I would watch a terribly interesting drama on the stage and ask myself, What are these people doing? Why are they doing it? How is this going to end?

"I want you to know about Kurt," Gerald said to me, "but I . . . I don't want you to be hurt. By this time you know it's nothing personal."

I smiled. "Sure. Nothing personal. Tell me about this wonderful guy."

Gerald blushed. "Well, he is wonderful. This may be hard for you to believe, but we don't even have a physical relationship yet. We're taking it real slow. We want to make it work."

A few days later Gerald called me on the phone. "Would you mind if I brought Kurt out to do yard work on Saturday? He's from a farm and he says he misses yard work. Can you believe anybody missing yard work? We could do some of the heavier stuff that I couldn't do alone."

I paused while I computed what he was asking. Did I want to meet Kurt? Not especially, but I was curious. Would the children think anything was unusual? They were so used to a stream of strangers coming through our home that I doubted they would think anything of it. But Kurt was . . . a homosexual. Well, last week one of my own homosexual friends had visited, had stayed overnight, and had taken us all out for a pancake breakfast.

"I suppose that would be all right," I heard myself say. "I guess I wouldn't mind."

"Good. He's wanted to meet you. And the kids. He's got a younger brother and sister in Kansas he hasn't seen for six years."

I liked Kurt. He was a tall, thin young man of about twenty-five, shy and gentle. From the kitchen window I watched Kurt and Gerald working and talking and laughing as they pulled weeds and repaired the fence and supervised the work of the children. I was amazed. I should be *hating Kurt,* I told myself. There was Gerald with his boyfriend on my property and I was allowing it! They were actually out there with my children! It probably would not look proper to anybody else, and I would not allow Gerald to bring a friend out very often even if he wanted to, but strangely, today, it was okay. I was past the point of wanting Gerald that way myself. I never thought of him anymore as a lover, a husband in that physical sense.

After the work was done we barbecued chicken for dinner and ate on the back deck. The children were at their most entertaining, and I watched both men looking at them in delight. As they were about to leave, Kurt asked for an aspirin.

"I've got a headache. Not used to all that sun, I guess."

"Here, sit down," I said. "I am known far and wide for getting rid of headaches."

I put my hands on the back of his head and massaged the pressure points at the base of the skull. Ever since I had learned the technique I had gotten rid of dozens of headaches of friends and even of strangers. I had once asked the service station attendant who was filling my car with gas if he had a headache, he was looking so miserable. He had. I got out of the car and worked on his head for two minutes and he thought I had worked a miracle. Why not work a miracle for Kurt? He was just a guy with a headache. A guy with a headache in my home.

After a few minutes he shook his head and blinked and said, "Hey, that's great. That's really great. It's gone!"

That night Gerald called me on the phone.

"Blossom? I just wanted to tell you thanks for letting Kurt come out. He's having to work through some really hard stuff right now and he misses his family terribly. They said he can come home for Christmas if he has his life cleaned up and isn't gay anymore. In the car on the way home, he cried. He was so moved that you would let him come out and see the kids and be so nice to him. Thanks."

A couple of weeks later in Relief Society the president passed around a petition that was being sponsored by another religious organization to be sent to President Carter urging his disapproval of any legislation in behalf of homosexuals. I passed the petition to the next woman without signing it. The petition also called for a day of prayer that these misled individuals might be "brought back into the light." A day of prayer. Oh, a day of prayer. I could do that. Certainly I could. I could give one more day of prayer.

I continued to hear about Kurt from time to time. Anyone overhearing our conversations would have thought it odd, I'm sure, that Gerald and I could discuss his relationships, but somehow the shift in our own relationship permitted it and it was okay. We seemed sometimes brother and sister and sometimes mother and son. After a few months I learned that Gerald had stopped seeing Kurt.

"I found that more and more I was being his father," Gerald said. "I didn't want that. I want an equal relationship with someone who can pull his own weight."

A few months later Gerald was talking about Steve, a fellow chorus member. Gerald was approaching the relationship cautiously, but he had high hopes for it. Steve was currently between jobs and staying with friends until he could get a place of his own. Gerald was tempted to invite him to move in with him while he was getting his life together, but decided that would not be good for the relationship. He wanted to be an equal, not a provider. I did not meet Steve, but watched the dynamics from across the Bay Bridge.

One Saturday, Gerald came in from helping the boys finish a go-cart they had been building together, and sat down on the couch.

"Guess what, Blossom? Last night I sent Steve packing."

"You did? Why?"

"At least for a while, until he gets his life in shape. Until he gets a decent job, gets an apartment of his own, and stops staying up until four every night getting stoned. I've been the only strong, stable thing in his life, and it's gotten to be too draining. Why do you suppose I keep drawing to me dependent people?"

When I told Gerald that Mario was coming to visit us, he was apprehensive. Mario had been best man at our wedding and Gerald still had a great love for him. But he knew Mario would disapprove of what he was doing, and felt that perhaps he wouldn't even try to understand it. Mario and Dana now had six children and he held a high position in the Church in Chicago. After their visit in the city, Mario came out to see me.

"How did he seem to you?" I asked as we walked in the hills near my home.

"He didn't look good," Mario said. "He's looking older than he should. Have you noticed?"

"I've noticed."

"Oh, it was hard." Mario heaved a great sigh. "Gerald talked nonstop about how happy he is and how much he's learning."

"Did you believe him?"

"Not entirely. He's chosen a position now that he has to defend."

"Chosen? Okay, Mario, just how much of all this did Gerald choose?"

"Not his homosexuality. I don't believe he chose that. That part just came. Homosexuality is not a sin. But unchastity is. I know people who are as homosexual as Gerald is who have made other choices and are working out very satisfactory family lives."

"Have they changed? Really changed?"

"Changed. Adapted. Made deliberate choices. I don't know. But there is more than one way to deal with all of this. I love Gerald. You know that. I've always considered him a very great man. He taught me some of the most important things I've ever learned. I have thought about him—about both of you—at least once a day for the last ten years. But everything he was telling me about having to follow the 'real' him . . . I don't know, I just can't buy that. Listen. I have watched someone close to me go with 'the real him' all his life. And in order to be 'true to himself' he destroyed lots of other people along the way. Sacrifice is sometimes not a bad principle. Sometimes it leads not to death but to life. When you don't 'follow the music that's in you,' if there's a noble reason for putting it away, maybe you will find an even richer music. I will always love Gerald, but his light is not as clear as it once was. He's dealing with a lot of sadness and guilt and confusion. I'm sorry."

"Oh, Mario, it's so complicated," I said wearily. "What do I do?"

"Just what you're doing. Love him. Protect yourself. Protect the children. Gerald is reaching for the light in his own way. One of the important things I've learned over these years is that everything that we call 'deviant behavior' is in some strange way a reaching for the light. Just love him."

Gerald did not tell me about Mark until they had been seeing each other for a couple of months. He did not want to be premature. And when he did tell me, I sensed a certain reluctance.

"It seems so strange to say this to you, but . . . I love him. I mean, I am really in love with him. It is all the excitement, all the romance, and all the crazy, wonderful stuff that being in love is supposed to be. And he's a good person. Really a good, sensitive, kind person. I am so happy. So happy!"

I nodded my head. "I can deal with that, Gerald. I want you to be happy. When do I get to meet this incredible person?"

Gerald laughed. "I've told him all about you, and he

read two of your poetry books. He already thinks you're wonderful. Next week the chorus is performing in Grace Cathedral. It's going to be a real event. We're singing my song, the words that I wrote to a piece by Sibelius. I want you to come. Mark will meet you out front with a ticket and you can sit with him. Will you?"

Bizarre. *Will this story never cease getting more and more bizarre*, I wondered. I should go and sit in Grace Cathedral with Gerald's lover and listen to the San Francisco Gay Men's Chorus perform a song he wrote? Why not? It would make another good entry in my diary.

I met Mark at the appointed place and we smiled and shook hands. I had ceased looking for monsters and perverts. I knew I would meet a cultured, pleasant, charming person, and I did. He had dark blond hair, a mustache, was tall and looked poetic somehow.

"Carol Lynn? I am really happy to meet you."

"Hi, Mark. Sorry I'm late. The train got stuck again."

We hurried to our seats and hardly had time to speak again before the program started. Mayor Feinstein spoke for a minute, saying how proud the city was of the accomplishments of its gay community and how we must all continue to work toward understanding and tolerance.

Then the music began with the chorus singing Gerald's lyric from the balcony. In front of me was the beautiful red-and-blue stained glass of the cathedral. At my side was my former husband's lover. And behind me was Gerald's voice and Gerald's words:

> Surely, surely, from the silence,
> Breaks the song that we never sang,
> Come the words that we never spoke,
> The love that we've always hidden.
>
> Once all men feared so to say it,
> The love that dared not speak its name.

At last, long last from the silence
Lovers come bringing gifts of song.

Voices sing of manly love.
No more will we hush the singing.
Never more will we hide our love.
No more will our joy be silenced.

Manly love has its melody.
Lovers too have a song to sing.

As the chorus took their places at the front, I was aware that Mark was looking for Gerald, just as I was. A soft smile was on his face and his eyes shone.

In the middle of "Amazing Grace" I found tears in my eyes. Nuts! I thought I was through with crying. "I once was lost, but now am found, was blind, but now can see." Oh, who is lost and who is found? I knew so little anymore. Gerald felt that he used to be lost and was now found. Others were certain that he is lost now and may be lost forever. Again, for a few moments, all the deep feelings I had for Gerald, feelings I had put away in an act of self-preservation, flooded over me. I didn't want Gerald to be lost and blind. I wanted him to see and to be happy. A cathedral seemed an appropriate place to pray. *Please take us all through the dangers and the snares and lead us safely home—Gerald and me and the children and Mark and all the men who are singing.*

Within a few weeks Mark had moved into the house Gerald was renting. All was going well, he said. But after they'd been domiciled together for a month and Gerald told me that Mark's snoring was driving him crazy, I could not stop laughing. Snoring! Oh, the pitfalls of love!

One Saturday as I picked up Gerald from the BART station, I noticed that he looked unusually drawn and weary.

"What's the matter, kid?" I asked.

"Oh," he sighed. "Life. Things. Mark moved out on Wednesday."

"Why?" I was honestly surprised.

"He couldn't take what he called my 'spaciness,' all my meditating and my spiritual study. He wanted to smoke a joint and watch television every night. I can't do that. You know I can't do that."

"Of course not."

"He was jealous of all my projects. He wanted all my attention. I can't live like that."

"Oh, Gerald. I'm sorry." It was true. I really was sorry. If Gerald had to follow the life he had chosen, I would much rather he have one relationship than many.

He was cheerful for the children. Gerald was never too depressed or weary to be cheerful for the children. But after they were in bed, we sat down to talk.

"So you're learning stuff, aren't you, Gerald?"

"Yep, I guess I am. But I sure wish I'd learn it fast. I don't want to do this many more times. Go ahead and laugh if you want to."

"I don't want to laugh. I want you to be happy. You know that."

"I know. Oh, it is so *hard to* find somebody who has just got the basic ingredients of maturity and loyalty and patience and concern. Why did Mark handle this so immaturely? He wasn't even willing to talk about it. While I was gone he just packed up and left. That was so immature!"

"Sounds like it. I'm sorry, Gerald."

"Oh, Blossom . . . if I could just find a man like you I'd be in seventh heaven!"

The words startled me into a laugh. I looked at Gerald, but he was not laughing. There were tears in his eyes.

Chapter 12

When Gerald cut his hair extremely short in deference to the current gay men's fashion, I was appalled.

"Gerald!" I exclaimed, as I picked him up at the BART station. "Why did you *do* that? It looks awful!"

"I think it looks sharp."

"You look like a skinned rabbit. And you do *not* think it looks sharp. You just did it because all the rest of the guys are doing it. This is high school stuff! Where is that wonderful rebel in you that dares to be different?"

I tried not to look at him for the rest of the day. He had been so handsome with a full head of blond hair. When I drove him back to the train that night I said, "Good night, Private Pearson."

"Hmm?"

"You look like you're in the Army. Take care of yourself."

Again I watched the lights of the train disappear into the distance. *The Army*, I thought. He did look like he was in the Army. And what a strange army. Thousands of men who have rejected the traditional male institutions have built a counterculture army of their own. Where is the sergeant who is calling out all these orders? Who says you have to cut your hair so you look like a skinned rabbit? Who says you have to wear the standard uniform, the plaid shirt and the tight Levi's? Who says you have to put more money than you can manage into keeping the body beautiful? Who says you have to subscribe to the newspapers in which men advertise their sexual specialties? Where is the sergeant who demands that you march to a certain rhythm and chant certain words? Just as, when I first met Gerald, I had wanted to storm Fort Ord and take Sergeant Saunders by the throat, I now wanted even more passionately to storm San Francisco and take by the throat whoever was in charge of this newest masculine mess. "I am a man!" they shout at Fort Ord, marching and waving their bayonets. "I am a man!" they shout in San Francisco, marching and waving their banners. Where there are armies there is usually destruction. And the women stay home as women always have and watch and wait to pick up the pieces.

I watched Gerald fall into step and I cursed the unseen sergeant of Castro Street.

We had these encounters, but my life was not centered on watching Gerald's new life unfold. It was centered on my children, my work, and my friends. Friends, long-standing and new, women and men, were always there to share my adventures and projects—to comfort me when I fell off an absurd pair of platform sandals and broke my foot, or to congratulate me when I performed the unlikely feat of rappelling down a mountain with my children.

Work was a vital nourishment. Writing a novel for young people based on pioneer-Indian history, reading it chapter by chapter to my children, having John say, "And then what? That's all you've got? Mom, get to that typewriter!"—that nourished me. Or speaking to groups of Mormon women, moving them with a new book of poems or hearing them explode with laughter at one of the entries in my series of humorous notebooks—"Interview Sister G. to find out why she's still depressed. Visit their trailer and talk to each of her twelve children to see if they know. (If not, call her husband in Alaska for his opinion)"—that nourished me.

Even though my relationship to Gerald was often more confusing than nourishing, it was part of the landscape of my life. Often he was the first one I needed to tell when something happened. "Guess what, kid?" I would say excitedly into the telephone, "I have really arrived! Today Ann Landers' column carried one of my poems—'author unknown.'" Gerald was the first one I showed the college textbook that anthologized three of my poems on the same pages with Keats and Frost. He was the first one I called with the news that I had won first place in the Bay Area Poet's competition. And to tell a joke that only he could really appreciate. And to describe how Emily had wowed everybody with her singing at the Church program, and how John had won a boa constrictor in a raffle.

When Gerald told me about Charles, I didn't take it too seriously. Charles was a very affluent physical therapist who thought that Gerald was the best thing that had ever happened to him. After Gerald had used up the money he'd received for selling his interest in the restaurant, he was broke and took several temporary jobs just to get by. Charles wanted to support Gerald for a year while he took time to do some writing he had been longing to do, and Gerald decided it was his turn to do something for himself. He moved into the beautiful Victorian house that Charles owned.

When Gerald started talking about Dan, I was confused.

"Who's Dan?" I asked. "Aren't you still with Charles?"

"Only as roommates. The other didn't work out for us. All we've been is roommates."

"So tell me about Dan."

Gerald smiled. "Blossom, I know you have heard this before, but this time it is really different. This time it is the *real thing.* Dan is . . . he's wonderful. You'll like him. He's brilliant. He read every page in the *Encyclopedia Britannica* before he was out of high school. You can't ask him a question that he doesn't know the answer to. And he sees all the things in me that I want someone to see. And—this will interest you, Blossom—he's a monogamist. He wants a committed, exclusive relationship. He wants—don't laugh—a 'marriage.'"

"Congratulations. Can I be bridesmaid?"

Gerald laughed. "Smart aleck. He really wants to meet you, but he's nervous about it. He bought three tickets for the opera next week and wants to take us both."

I went to the opera. I met Dan and I liked him. He was of medium height, dark-haired, slight of build and had a modest, almost self-effacing manner. The opera was billed as a feminist piece and featured the words of Emily Dickinson, Virginia Woolf, Isadora Duncan, and Gertrude Stein. I found it boring and was glad when the final curtain came down. Discovering that it was raining outside, Gerald suggested he get the car and drive back for Dan and me. As Dan and I stood in the foyer waiting, I searched for some appropriate thing to say. In a moment I found it.

"Well," I said, smiling directly into Dan's eyes, "I hear you want to marry my husband."

Dan blushed and stammered, and I thought for a moment that he might turn and run. Then he laughed. "Well, yes, it's true. I love Gerald very much. He's a very special person. But I don't need to tell you that."

"No, you don't. I suppose you know I love Gerald very much too. He's terribly important to me. I like you, Dan. Strange as it seems, I'd like you and Gerald to have a long and happy life together. Take good care of him."

Dan nodded and his face filled with emotion. "Thanks, Carol Lynn. That means a lot to me." Then he gave me a quick embrace. "Thanks," he said again.

When Gerald next came to visit, I sat him down like a concerned parent to talk. "Listen, kid," I said, "I have a feeling in my heart that if you can't make it work with Dan, you can't make it work with anybody. Are you prepared to take this seriously?"

"Very seriously."

"Gerald, do you know what's wrong with the gay community?"

"Well, I've got my own list and it's pretty long. What's on yours?"

"Nobody ever has to work on a relationship. With men and women there's marriage. There's the legal stuff. There are the children. When a problem comes up, you think twice before you call it quits. You work on it long and hard before you give up."

"Hey, Blossom, you're not telling me one thing I don't know. In the gay community when a problem comes up, it's just too easy to junk the relationship and move on to the next person. I know that. I've seen that. I've done that. Just around the corner or in the next bar will be somebody who can take away all the hurt, and you can start all over again. But then that one gets complicated. You ain't tellin' me nuthin', Blossom."

I sighed. "Oh, Gerald, I don't want to see you grow old still looking for your true love."

Gerald shrugged. "And if I do? Isn't the journey better than the destination? Romance keeps you young."

Every time I saw a newspaper account of violence toward homosexuals, I became fearful and asked Gerald again if he was doing everything possible to protect himself. A homosexual man had been killed in a beating by four young men screaming, "Faggot! Faggot!" They'd had nothing to do on a Saturday night and had gone out "gay bashing" for fun. And on the East Coast a young homosexual man had been thrown to his death from a bridge.

Nothing really violent had ever happened to Gerald.

One evening as he was leaving the school where the chorus rehearsed and was about to cross the street, a pickup truck with three teenagers in it sped by. The one closest to him spat at him and shouted something foul and laughed. On the night he told me that, it was hard for me to sleep. Our old friend Sam, who had told me the story of his shock therapy, had not been so fortunate. He called one evening to see how I was doing, and I invited him to come out for a visit. Sam was living in San Francisco now, said he was happy, belonged to a square-dancing club and had some good community involvement.

"But there's been some bad stuff," he said, "some really bad stuff. A couple of years ago I was coming out of a place that was known as a gay hangout, and I started walking down the sidewalk. Suddenly a hand stopped me and turned me around. There was this crowbar raised above my head. The next thing I knew my whole face exploded. Two young guys were running away laughing. Somebody got me to the hospital. It took five major surgeries to put my face together."

"Oh, Sam, I'm sorry. Hey, it looks great. It really does."

Sam smiled. "That's seventy thousand dollars in plastic surgery you're lookin' at there. They had to completely reconstruct the left side of my face. And how do you like my new eye?"

"It's glass?"

"Yep. Looks pretty good, huh?"

"I would never have known. Oh, Sam, I'm sorry."

Sam shrugged. "Some have gotten worse."

"Just one more thing I wanted to ask. They're not still doing shock therapy at BYU, are they?"

"No, they're not. From what I hear they're a lot more realistic now, a lot more understanding. I'm glad."

On a December afternoon four years after the divorce, Emily and I were having a conflict. She was fourteen and was emerging as a new person every day, certain that she had life all figured out and that her mother knew precious little about even less.

"Emily, just be patient," I pleaded. "There are some things about all this that you don't know about. Someday you will understand a lot more about me, about the divorce, about—"

"I understand more than you think I do, Mom. I know why you and Gerald got a divorce." Gerald had asked Emily to call him by his first name and all the children did it now.

I looked at her cautiously, "Why?"

"Because Gerald's gay."

I was stunned. She had said it so matter-of-factly, very much like she would have said, "Gerald's five feet ten."

"How did you know that, Emily?"

"I'm not dumb. I figured it out. And the boys know too."

I did not have to tell the children to love Gerald anyway. It would never have occurred to them not to love him. They had all accepted this new piece of information unemotionally. I spoke to each of them privately, telling the whole story from my point of view and letting them ask any questions they wanted to ask. Later on, Gerald spoke to each of them privately and told them the story of his life, what all this meant and what it did not mean.

"John, what do you think?" I said one evening when he and I were alone. "Do you think you're going to grow up to be gay?"

"No, I don't think so," he said. "Do you think I am?"

"No. Have you thought what it might be like?"

"Yeah. I've thought about it, but the idea of being with girls feels better to me."

"Don't let it worry you, John. Being gay is not inherited. I don't think it's something you're going to have to deal with. You're going to be a good husband and a good dad and you're going to be very happy."

I had similar conversations with Aaron and also with Emily.

Once when Gerald was visiting and Emily was carrying on dramatically about her latest disappointment with the boy she had a current crush on, she exploded, "That does it! I am through with boys! I'm going to become a *lesbian nun!*"

I laughed. Gerald laughed and then sobered up instantly.

"Oh, Emily," he said, "that is not what you want. Believe me that is not what you want. Don't even *say* that. I'm sure there are many lesbians who are nice people, but if you can be straight, do it. Being a homosexual is a very difficult life. Anybody who would volunteer for it is crazy."

In a serious talk on the subject, Gerald quizzed me as to what I would do in the unlikely possibility that one of our children might turn out to be gay.

"Well," I said, "I would do everything possible to steer them away from it. I would encourage therapy, no matter how unsuccessful it might be. I would stress that there are always choices. I would try to show them that you don't have to act on every impulse that you have—you don't hit somebody in the nose every time you get angry—and you don't have sex every time you get turned on. But whatever they chose, I would still love them. Of course I would still love them."

Gerald was silent for a moment, then said, "That's a secret fear that I've had, that one of the children might be gay and you couldn't handle it, you couldn't still love them."

"Gerald, you're crazy! Don't I still love *you?*"

Gerald nodded. "And it always surprises me."

It may have been the children's chicken pox that precipitated Gerald's case of shingles. It was a horrendously painful case, and he was hospitalized with a fifty-fifty chance of losing his left eye. As soon as I found out, I went to Presbyterian Hospital in San Francisco. Dan was there at his bedside, and they both were pleased to see me when I walked in the door.

"Oh, Blossom. You didn't have to come."

"Sure, I did," I said, kissing the side of his face that did not have a bandage over the eye. "Wouldn't you come if I were in the hospital?"

"Of course."

"How do you feel?"

"It hurts like hell."

We visited about an hour and I told Gerald all my latest jokes, until he asked me to stop because laughing made his face hurt even more. Dan drove me to BART and we sat together in the darkened car sharing a strange bond. We both loved Gerald and we both wanted him to be well. Dan and I had gotten to be quite good friends over the previous several months. I had invited him out for Thanksgiving dinner along with a variety of other people I knew who did not have families. And he had called me to give me greetings on my birthday. Thinking about it, I knew it was strange, but feeling about it, I knew it was okay.

A faithful Mormon would send for the Elders and request a priesthood blessing, but I knew that would not interest Gerald. We said our customary prayers for Gerald's health, but I also decided to make a telephone call to a spiritual healer whose seminar I had attended at John F. Kennedy University in Orinda. Olga Worrall was perhaps the country's most studied psychic or spiritual healer. I had seen her on several television documentaries, hooked up to machines that measured the flow of her energy as she sent out healing to a target patient. I believed in such things. My own great-grandfather, George Warren Sirrine, who founded Mesa, Arizona, was known throughout the West as a healer and was sent for to stop the flow of blood in people and in animals.

I asked Mrs. Worrall to put Gerald's name on her list of people to receive healing. She said she would and that the eye was going to be all right. She reminded me to join her in her nine o'clock prayer and meditation and to have Gerald do the same.

I told Gerald, and later that evening he called me on the telephone.

"Blossom?" His voice was shaking. "It was amazing. During the meditation the intense pain on the left side of my face turned into a warm tingling. It felt so good. For about half an hour it just tingled."

The next night at meditation time the children and I were visiting Gerald in his hospital room. We all meditated together and Gerald reported a similar experience. The pain had come back, but to a lesser extent, and during the meditation it again became a warm tingle. The following day he felt a lot better and the doctors reported that the damage to the eye had halted and his eyesight was no longer in danger.

For months Gerald remained weak. The doctors had given him massive doses of steroids and antibiotics and he seemed constantly drained of energy. I called him frequently and tried to cheer him up with stories about the children.

"Here's one you'll like, kid. You know how Aaron sometimes doesn't like to sleep alone. He says he gets freaked. The other night he was going around asking who would like to sleep in his room, and nobody was interested. John didn't want to. Katy didn't want to. Emily didn't want to. So they all went to their own rooms. Half an hour later, as I was shutting my door, I saw Aaron walking down the hall carrying Katy, fast asleep, into his room."

Gerald wanted to introduce me to computers. He had been working with one for an engineering firm for months and was certain that a word processor would be a major breakthrough in my writing. I went into the city one afternoon and met him after work, where he showed me how the computer edited copy like magic. And then he took me to dinner. Wonderful food could ordinarily make Gerald blissful, but this evening I sensed a strange melancholy.

"What's the matter, Gerald?" I finally ventured. "Troubles with Dan?"

"No. We're okay."

"Then what?"

Gerald was silent a moment, and then he put down his fork and leaned back. "Michael died."

"Michael? Charles's friend, who got you the job?"

Gerald nodded. "My supervisor at work. Such a good man."

"Gee, I'm sorry. What was it?"

Gerald folded his napkin and put it beside his plate. "AIDS," he said.

"AIDS? What's that?"

"It's a new disease. Acquired Immune Deficiency Syndrome. It destroys the immune system so you can't fight off anything. It mostly attacks gay men."

"Gay men? How can it single out gay men?"

"It's sexually transmitted."

"Oh." I stared at the flickering candle in the little red dish. "Gerald, are you . . . ? Do you think . . . ?"

"No, Blossom. I do not have AIDS. It's just this damn yeast infection. Everything they did to me for the shingles wiped out my defenses. When this yeast infection is over, I'll be fine."

"Are there tests you can have? Certainly if they catch it in an early stage the cure rate must be higher."

Gerald refolded his napkin and arranged the silverware on it carefully, one piece at a time. Then he looked at me. "Blossom, the cure rate for AIDS is zero."

I studied Gerald's face for a moment, then reached over and touched his hand. "Kid, are you being careful?"

Gerald nodded. "Completely. Dan and I are totally monogamous." He forced a laugh. "You'll like this, Blossom. It's scaring the hell out of the whole gay community. For the sane ones, party time is over. And for the crazy ones the party gets crazier—you may already have it, so play with what time you've got left."

I was silent as the waiter brought the bill and Gerald reached for his wallet. We should have sat away from the door. I always got cold in restaurants, and right now, even through my sweater, my arms felt chilled.

"Don't worry about this, Blossom," Gerald smiled as he stood up. "As soon as this yeast infection goes away, I'll be fine."

I watched the papers. From time to time there was an article about this mysterious new disease. At that time, besides male homosexuals, its known victims were hemophiliacs who had frequent blood transfusions, drug abusers who shared contaminated needles, and unaccountably, a small number of Haitians. Predictably AIDS jokes began to surface. "Do you know the hardest part of having AIDS? Convincing your mother that you're Haitian." That was the only one I found funny.

The disease baffled everyone. The medical establishment had never seen anything like it and they stood by helpless. Doctors and researchers gave their best efforts and met only with frustration. From the limited information then available I tried to piece together any possible dangers to me and to the children. There were definite indications that the disease could not be spread by casual contact, even by living in the same house with someone who had it. Newspaper articles said that no health care worker had to that time contracted AIDS through routine care of the sick. Nevertheless, with all of the unknowns about AIDS, fear was escalating. Even back then, before there was quite so much hysteria about the disease, men who were diagnosed with AIDS sometimes came back to their apartments to find their belongings piled on the doorstep. They had become society's new lepers.

"Blossom," Gerald's voice was tight as he asked me the question. "I don't think I've got AIDS, but we both know I'm not well. Are you going to ask me not to come out anymore?"

I looked at Gerald quietly as thoughts chased one another through my mind. If there were real danger to the children, I would do anything to protect them, even ban their father. If the disease could be contracted from casual contact, we were already in trouble, but I had prayed and studied about it, and felt that we were not in danger. How could the children bear not seeing Gerald anymore? And how could he bear not seeing us? I could not do that to him.

"No, Gerald," I replied. "I'm not going to ask you to stay away. We're family. We will always be family. The only thing I've decided to ask is that until we know more about all this you not kiss the children."

"I haven't been. I won't. Thanks, Blossom."

I always remembered our wedding anniversary. Every September 9, I woke up and thought about that beautiful autumn day in Utah. Many leaves had fallen since then. My own life had been through season after season of things dying and fluttering down and new green appearing. Life was insistent. And September 9 kept coming around. That morning I called Gerald at work.

"Hi, kid," I said. "Happy anniversary!"

"Smart aleck," Gerald laughed. "Will you never stop being a smart aleck?"

"Hey, I'm not being a smart aleck. I just wanted to call and tell you that in spite of everything, I'm not sorry I married you. I've been adding up the credits and the debits all morning and I find there are too many good things in my life that I would not have had without you. So there. Happy anniversary, Gerald."

The next day when he came out, he brought me a card and a bouquet of flowers, pink and purple good wishes purchased from a San Francisco street vendor. Gerald often brought me cards for birthdays, Mother's Days, and Valentine's Days. This one proclaimed in bold red script, "You're wonderful and I love you." To that he had added, "Thanks for your strength, your love, your talent and beauty—and your contribution to eighteen years of my life—love, Gerald."

Over the next couple of months Gerald claimed to be feeling somewhat better, but I did not see it. I saw a man who looked thinner and had deeper lines in his face and who seemed constantly preoccupied. In December, however, he arrived for his Saturday visit bursting with enthusiasm. He had quit his job with the engineering firm and was going to work as an independent contractor, doing the same kind of computer work for more than three times the money.

"I should get sixty thousand dollars a year," he beamed at dinner. "And it's about time. I'm sick of being poor, sick of not being able to give you guys what you deserve. This first job will last six weeks and my agent says there should be plenty more after it. If this goes well, I'm going to take you all to Hawaii next summer."

"Wow!" said John, "Hawaii! Even Mom?"

"Of course even Mom, if she wants to go. Oh, this is such a relief. My karma's changing. I know it is!"

We did not see much of Gerald during those six weeks. The woman who had contracted him to work had mapped out, he said, an impossible request. He would have to work night and day to meet her deadline, and even so, he wasn't sure he could do it. But she was adamant. Gerald knew that his whole future depended on doing this first job right. He would do it if it killed him.

"Gerald, that cough does not sound good," I said to him on one of my calls.

"I know," he said, "I'm not getting enough sleep. That's all. Just two more weeks. I'll be okay."

"Gerald, this is crazy."

"I know. I hate it. We sell our souls to mammon. But right now mammon is the name of the game and I've got to play it."

"Oh, Gerald, you should not even be in computers. You should do anything else—be a street-corner philosopher, sell home-bound copies of your poems for a dollar each, teach classes in meditation, work in a 'new age' bookstore. Anything but computers. What's feeding your soul? Nothing!"

Gerald sighed. "You're right, Blossom, but I am so sick of being poor. There is so much I want to do. If I can just hang on, I'll be okay."

"Take care of yourself," Gerald," I said. "You know, you need a wife to take care of you." I had often joked with Gerald that he needed a wife for this or a wife for that. But this time I was not laughing.

Gerald was not laughing either.

"Something else I wanted to tell you," he went on. "Dan told me today that the guy he lived with two years ago just died of AIDS."

"And Dan?" I asked cautiously.

"The tests show he's got what they call pre-AIDS. But it doesn't necessarily develop into the full-blown syndrome. He's got swollen glands, but the doctor said that was a good sign."

"Gerald? You haven't been talking much about Dan. Are you still seeing him?"

After a pause, Gerald spoke. "He smothers me. He drains me. No, we're not seeing much of each other."

"Gerald." The words sounded so futile as I said them, so like speaking into a storm. "Take care of yourself."

Christmas of 1983 was lovely, one of the best I can remember. Gerald came out on Christmas Eve, as he always did, and spent the night and Christmas Day with us. His exhaustion was relieved by the children's enthusiasm. After going to see the movie *Yentl,* we watched the Sing-It-Yourself *Messiah* on television, a thrilling event featuring five thousand lay singers who had gathered to sing with a professional orchestra and conductor.

"Shall we do that next year?" Gerald said to the kids. "Shall we study the score of *The Messiah* and sing with them? I'd love that."

Then I read "Why the Chimes Rang," my favorite Christmas story. My mother had read it to us when I was little and Christmas was never real to me until I had read the story aloud. It had come to be an expected part of our Christmas Eve ritual. My voice always broke a little toward the end when the long-silent bells finally ring for the gift of the little gold piece sent by Pedro, who missed the Christmas festival to stay outside the city walls in the snow caring for a dying woman he had stumbled upon.

After that I read Henry Van Dyke's "The Other Wise Man," the classic story of the Magi who misses the journey to Bethlehem and spends the treasures he was going to give to the Christ child to save those he meets along the way. When he is dying as a very old man, unsuccessful in his quest to find the King, he hears a voice telling him he has already given his gift to the Lord. He does not understand and replies, "Not so, my Lord! For when saw I thee an hungered and fed thee? Or thirsty, and gave thee drink? When saw I thee a stranger, and took thee in? Or naked, and clothed thee? When saw I thee sick or in prison, and came unto thee?"

The voice comes again. "Verily I say unto thee, Inasmuch, as thou hast done it unto one of the least of these my brethren, thou hast done it unto me."

Gerald sat on the couch with his arms around two of the children and his eyes were moist when I finished reading. Then he spoke.

"I have something for our Christmas program, too," he said. "I want to lead you in a meditation for peace. Close your eyes, everybody. Feel the energy that is in you, giving you life. Now feel and visualize that energy rising out of you and joining with the energy of all of us together in this room. It is a great, glowing mass of energy, of spirit, and rises further now and joins with the energy of everybody everywhere who are doing positive things. Now all that energy rises and is joined by the brightest, the most powerful energy of all, that of Christ, and as our light and energy joins with his, there is a force that is shining and powerful. Now I want you to visualize this great and powerful light moving across the entire world. Wherever it meets war, wherever it meets hate, wherever it meets prejudice, it moves through it and dissolves it and leaves only peace and love. See it move everywhere, across the entire planet, until there is truly peace on earth."

The meditation took several minutes. When it was through we sat still for a while and watched the flames lick gold in the fireplace. After the children were sent to bed, Gerald and I filled the stockings, as we always did. The soft lights of the tree were reflected in the glass panes of the French doors, and the Christmas voices of Barbra Streisand and the Mormon Tabernacle Choir sang in the background. I brought down the four guitars that were this year's Santa Claus presents and we arranged them carefully around the room. We drank the cocoa and took a bite out of the cookie that Katy had left for Santa beside the fireplace.

"Let's do that," said Gerald as we sat alone together by the fire. "Next year let's go sing *The Messiah.*"

Three months later, at the end of March, Gerald called me on the telephone. "Blossom? They completed all the tests. I've got AIDS."

Chapter 13

Three days later, on the evening we had selected to tell the children, I drove down to pick up Gerald at the BART station. Driving the car was a comforting thing to do—driving the car and defrosting the refrigerator and shopping for groceries. The automatic, the essential, the familiar keep your mind in acceptable territory, keep it from plunging too far into new and terrifying knowledge. Gerald had AIDS. The fact washed over me a hundred times a day like a cold ocean wave. I stopped for the stop sign at Buena Vista Avenue, made sure the truck was safely past, turned the steering wheel to the right, pushed the gas pedal, and then felt the wave hit me again. Gerald had AIDS.

As I arrived at the station, there he was on his usual bench, legs crossed, reading his well-worn paperback copy of *Leaves of Grass*. I had given him a deluxe edition of the book a couple of years ago when I had finally forgiven Walt Whitman, but Gerald preferred his paperback copy of the poems and carried it around in his red traveling bag. He stood up and smiled as he saw my rundown yellow Volvo station wagon. The day was sunny, but he wore a coat. He always wore a coat these days; his body was not keeping him warm enough. His hair had not grown since I had seen him the week before. I had been watching his hair. It had simply stopped growing.

"Hi, Gerald." I stepped out of the car and embraced him. This was the first I'd seen him since he gave me the news, although we had talked several times on the phone.

"Hi, Blossom." Gerald put into the back of the car the carefully wrapped painting he had asked me to take back to Utah on my next trip. He had arranged for Trevor, the artist, to resell it. It could bring close to two thousand dollars and Gerald needed the money badly. He had not been well enough to work since January, when he had nearly killed himself finishing the computer job. And because he had gone from a payroll position to being self-employed, he was denied state disability.

"How you doing, kid?" I asked, as he settled into the front seat beside me.

"Tired," he said. He had been tired for months, his sleep disturbed by uncomfortable night sweats and chills.

But Gerald smiled. Much of his light was still there. I could deal with his death, if that had to be. But if all his light went out before then—just went out on its own—how could I bear it?

The children were in a production of *Oliver* at Emily's high school that evening, and we planned to talk to them after the performance, when supper was finished, Gerald pulled out a large envelope and handed it to Emily.

"Ta dum!" He smiled broadly.

"My pictures!" Emily gasped.

I watched Gerald watch Emily as she opened the envelope. He looked so happy, so pleased at her pleasure as she took out the pictures and we "oohed" and "aahed" at them. Emily had known since age three that she wanted to be a performer, and Gerald had done everything his modest finances would allow to promote her dream. He had taken her to see Diana Ross and others in concert and talked to Emily for hours about finding and expressing her own uniqueness. A few months ago he had arranged a photography session with his good friend John Chidester, who was on the brink of making it big. Gerald was driven in his need to do this for Emily. They spent a whole day with a professional makeup person, hairdresser and costumer and took over five hundred shots. John had raved over how easily and beautifully Emily gave to the camera, and Gerald had not been able to come down to earth for days. So much—so much he had not been able to give Emily. But this *he would* give her. The pictures were stunning.

"Oh, Gerald," Emily fell into his arms. "Oh, thank you!"

"You're welcome, sweetheart." Gerald's voice was choked.

Emily grabbed the pictures to show the boys and Katy.

"Gerald," I said when she had gone, "how did you pay for those pictures? You said it would take five hundred dollars before you could have the prints."

"I managed."

"You haven't been eating, have you, Gerald? You spent the last of your money on those pictures."

"Well? They're more important than food right now. I'll be okay. By next week I should have food stamps."

"Gerald," I spoke slowly, "you're not going to be able to keep your apartment for long. I think that—how would you feel about coming out to stay with us?"

I had been thinking about it for three days now, since Gerald had told me the diagnosis was firm. I knew it was a strange offer. I knew that many on the outside would be shocked, would not approve. But I was not on the outside, I was on the inside, and so were Gerald and the children, and we were the only ones that really mattered. I had prayed about it. I had run it through the computer of my mind and my heart, and that was the answer that came out. It felt right.

"How would you feel about that, Gerald?" I repeated.

When Gerald spoke it was with difficulty. "Thanks.

Thanks, Blossom. You know how much that means to me. But not now. I'm . . . I'm not giving up. You know that. I'm going to fight this thing with everything I've got. And I'm going to beat it. Somehow, I'm going to beat it. I want to keep my apartment, at least for as long as possible. There should be some kind of assistance coming through. And I need to be a resident of the city in order to get the medical help they've set up. Thanks, Blossom."

I watched the play that night through Gerald's eyes. Katy sat on his lap. She had had the least benefit of a father of any of the children, and I always liked seeing them close, seeing Gerald hold her or listen to her piano pieces. What must it be like to hold your little girl on your lap and know that in your body courses a devastating disease? What must it be like to look at those two darling blond boys on the stage with the others singing, "Food, glorious food," shining brighter than the floodlights, and know that in a couple of hours you must tell them you have a fatal illness? What must it be like to hear that dear, compelling voice offstage that makes everyone in the audience lift their heads, and to see that tall, beautiful girl walk into the light carrying her basket of flowers and wonder if you will be here for the school play next spring?

"Who will buy this wonderful morning?" Gerald's face softened, and he looked at her adoringly. "Such a sky I never did see. Who will wrap it up with a ribbon, and put it in a box for me?" How do you hear those words from the daughter who loves you more than any other human being alive and gives you more reason for being than anyone else ever has? Who will buy this wonderful moment? Wrap it up tightly, safely, safely so it will stay forever. Put it in a box, a box you can hold and touch and take with you and open whenever you need it, always.

I put Katy to bed when we got home. She didn't need to know any of this. Gerald had told her that he was ill and would be going to the hospital for treatment. That was all an eight-year-old needed to know. Then the rest of us went up to my bedroom. Emily and Gerald sat together on the couch. John sprawled across my bed, and Aaron and I sat on the bed against the bolster pillow.

"Well, you guys," Gerald said, putting an arm around Emily and drawing her a little closer. "There's something I need to tell you. The doctors have finally figured out what's been causing all my problems." He paused. "I've got AIDS."

Emily closed her eyes and pinched her lips together. I tightened my arm around Aaron's shoulder, and in a moment I felt a wet drop on my hand. I could not see John's face. The children had all heard of the disease. Few people hadn't.

Emily's health class had spent a whole hour on it, and she had asked me that night, "Mom, Gerald couldn't . . . Gerald doesn't have AIDS, does he?" I had told her I hoped not.

Gerald continued. "I think all of you know what the disease means. It's pretty serious, but they're making progress all the time in finding an answer. I want you to know that I'm going to do everything I can to get well. I'm going into the hospital on Monday for a twenty-one-day treatment for pneumonia. I know several guys who have been through the treatment and are well again. So I don't want you to worry too much. I really believe I'm going to get well."

Emily turned and buried her face in her father's shoulder. "I love you, Gerald," she said.

"I love you too, Em, all of you. And you're going to help me get through this."

Emily nodded her head, her face still hidden, and all were silent.

"Of all the people who have this disease," I finally said, "no one has more to live for than Gerald does. Doctors and researchers are working night and day on finding a cure. And we'll do our part too. We'll continue our prayers. We'll meditate and visualize. Thoughts have a strong effect. And you remember Mr. Cousins' book that I told you about—how he cured himself of an unbeatable illness through laughter therapy? You've got to collect all the funny things that happen at school, all the jokes you hear, and pass them on to Gerald."

John spoke, his voice quavering. "In that book by Bette Midler that Gerald brought out, *Baby Divine,* she made herself well by laughing."

"You bet," Gerald said. "And if Baby Divine and Norman Cousins can do it, Gerald Pearson can do it."

"Now, before we put Gerald to bed," I said, "we've got to make him laugh. One good laugh before we close this day. Who's got a good joke?"

Everyone thought for a moment.

"Well, I have something funny," I said. "And this really happened. Aaron and Katy and I were in the kitchen today and Katy said something that didn't make any sense. Aaron laughed and said, 'Oh, I love it when Katy doesn't know what she's talking about, when she just chooses a word at ransom!'"

Gerald laughed, that wonderful laugh of his that always filled a room without any self-consciousness. His laugh ended in a cough, but still he smiled. "That's great," he said. "Ransom."

Gerald threw himself into getting well just like he had thrown himself into falling in love with me and into publishing *Beginnings* and into the projects that had come along since then. He read everything available. He even cut out his daily glass of wine because it evidently did not help support the immune system. He worked with a psychotherapist friend on exorcizing old mental patterns that were self-negating. There was a feeling in the gay community that there was a strong psychological component to this disease. Gerald faithfully meditated and wrote out in his notebooks his prescribed daily affirmations, such as "My immune system is getting stronger and stronger" and "I, Gerald, deserve perfect health, wealth, and love."

I watched Gerald fight for his life and I gave him every bit of support I could gather. I watched Don Quixote take his sword against this ultimate foe and I was moved with his bravery. "We create our own reality," Gerald had said for years. "All of this *means* something. We bring into our lives whatever we need in order to progress." And despite the horror of his illness, Gerald's philosophy did not change.

"Somehow I am responsible for this condition," he would say. "And now I have to figure out how to change my thinking so that I can create health instead of illness."

I expected Gerald to pull off a miracle. I really did. In spite of everything we had been through, in spite of all the confusions and problems I had seen, I continued to see something in Gerald that to me was almost supernatural. I kept a romanticized view of him even though the romance was gone. His gifts were so good. His desire to do something helpful was so deep. His dream of being part of the "transformation of consciousness" was so strong, I could not stop believing in him.

I developed a fantasy and held on to it determinedly. Gerald would get well. By the sheer force of his will and his spirit and perhaps some medical breakthroughs, Gerald would get well. In the process, whatever had been holding him back would be lifted and he would fulfill all his best dreams. He would be a light to point better directions to the gay community. And he would be the bridge he had so wanted to be to develop understanding of homosexuals to the larger world. He would take what he had been learning about what love really is and synthesize it into a wonderful message. He would write the things he only had reams of notes on. He would speak and people would listen. Surely that's what would happen. Surely Gerald would not die with his dreams unfulfilled. He had often quoted someone who said, "Most men die with their music still in them." Gerald had sung, but not all his songs. Not all. Surely there would be a miracle!

The children and I were faithful in our prayers and our healing meditations. Close friends and family were notified and asked for their prayers. Gerald's name was put on the prayer roll in two Mormon temples. Again I called Olga Worrall, the spiritual healer. What else, what other possible things could be done?

As the children and I took the elevator up to 5-B, the AIDS ward of San Francisco General Hospital, I pushed my face into the carnations we had bought where the bus stopped just across the street. I hated the smell of a hospital ever since my mother died.

We stepped off the elevator and walked toward Gerald's room. There were twelve beds in the AIDS ward and they were constantly full. Gerald had developed a new appreciation for San Francisco because of how it had mobilized itself to take care of AIDS victims. It was 1984, and thousands were afflicted across America, but media coverage had been minimal. "Our editors don't want gay stories," reporters had told the medical researchers. But when the disease appeared to be crossing sexual boundaries, and heterosexuals were threatened too, people were starting to take notice. The disease would soon be more than "the gay plague," and financing would come that should have been available several years earlier. But San Francisco had come through. The AIDS ward was staffed with carefully screened medical personnel and volunteers who were there because they *wanted* to be there. A volunteer organization called Shanti offered counseling, housekeeping, transportation, and some crisis financial help to AIDS victims. Social workers and many others formed a network of support. I felt a surge of gratitude toward every doctor, nurse, and aide I passed in the halls of 5-B.

"Hi, you guys!" Gerald beamed as we entered the room.

"You folks can stay, but the carnations have got to go," said the aide who was removing Gerald's supper tray. "We've got to control the bacterial environment carefully around here. You visitors are not at risk for catching AIDS, but the AIDS patients are at risk for catching *everything*. They're the ones we have to protect. I'll put these at the nurse's station and you can pick them up when you leave."

"Well, Gerald, your color looks great," I said brightly, as the aide left the room.

"Oh, I'm feeling a lot better," he said. "Good news too. Dr. Abrams said this stuff is clearing up my lungs so well that he'll just keep me for fourteen days instead of the usual twenty-one." Gerald gestured to the IV that was sending carefully measured drops into his blood stream. "My T-cells are up, which is the major good news, and I'm not as nauseated as I was. They're going to give me another blood transfusion tomorrow, which should help a lot. Then the next day I get to go home."

"Yay!" said Emily, clapping her hands.

"We've got about a hundred jokes for you," said John, grinning. "Are you ready?"

"I'm ready." Gerald smiled and leaned back on the hospital bed. His color was better. It really was.

"Do you know what happens when you don't pay your exorcist?"

"No, I don't. What happens?"

"You get repossessed."

Gerald laughed, and everything was all right. I knew that no one had been pronounced cured of AIDS. But Gerald was over the Pneumosystis carinii. His T-cells were up. They were letting him leave the hospital. He laughed because if you don't pay your exorcist, you get repossessed. Everything was all right.

The next day on the news came a report of a break-through in the treatment of both AIDS and cancer, a thing called interferon that essentially builds an artificial immune system. I called Gerald at the hospital immediately.

"Kid," I said, "did you hear the news about interferon?"

"Yes," he said. "Everybody here's talking about it. Isn't it great? In two or three months they should have it ready for experimental use, and Dr. Abrams said if I don't develop any new infections, I'll be a candidate for it."

"That's great, Gerald. That's really *great*! You can hang on for a couple of months!" I hung up the phone with a lighter heart than I'd had in weeks. I knew that the research-ers wouldn't let us down. And three weeks later when the headlines carried the news that the AIDS virus had been isolated, I breathed another sigh of relief. Any week now, any day now, they would announce the cure.

I wanted to accompany Gerald on one of his visits to the AIDS clinic, to meet his doctor and to ask questions. An entire floor of one of the buildings at San Francisco General had been converted to an AIDS clinic and already it had outgrown its home. That morning, we were told, the clinic had been packed, but now, late in the afternoon, there were only eight men in the waiting room.

I sat beside Gerald and studied the other men. They were all young, under forty, I judged. Two had come in with canes. Several had the lesions on their skin that indicated Kaposi's sarcoma, the cancer that so often manifested with AIDS. A young boy with curly red hair stared at the floor. A black man leaned against a larger man whose arm was around his shoulder.

A nurse called Gerald's name and we made our way to

a small examining room. He was weighed and blood was taken. Gerald had told me a lot about Dr. Abrams, and when he came in, I was surprised to see how young he was. He had been trained to treat cancer, so he was used to the possibility of death; but since taking charge of the AIDS program, all his patients were dying, *all* of them. These were men his own age to whom he could relate so well and for whom he could do so little. How he could spend every day dealing with the horror of this disease I could not fathom. His caseload would double every six to nine months. Surely he must be grateful, as I was, that AIDS was almost under control.

"Hi, Gerald," Dr. Abrams said, glancing up from the file he had been looking at as he came through the door. Then he noticed me.

"Dr. Abrams, I want you to meet Carol Lynn, my former wife."

Dr. Abrams and I exchanged greetings.

"We don't see many women around here," he said. "I've had a few patients come in with their mothers and a sister or two, but you're the first wife I've met."

"How does my blood look?" Gerald asked, anxious to get a report.

"Blood looks pretty good. Lungs look good. Weight's staying good. But . . ." Dr. Abrams paused and studied his files for a moment.

Gerald blew out his breath in a long sigh. "What's the bad news?"

"The bone marrow we sent in. They found tuberculosis in it. I was afraid of that. It's been showing up a lot."

"But there's a treatment for tuberculosis," I said. "You can treat it, can't you? Gerald responded well to the treatment for pneumonia."

"There's only a slim chance that it's the usual kind of tuberculosis for which there is treatment. Almost certainly it's one of the very rare forms that human beings aren't ordinarily affected by. The trouble is that someone who has no immune system can be invaded by lots of unusual things. We're sending specimens of T.B. back to the World Health Organization and being told they're brand new strains." The doctor closed the file and looked at us both. "Sorry the news isn't better."

"What about the artificial immune system?" I asked. "What about interferon?"

"Not much good news there either," he said. "The experimentation that's been done shows no real promise. It's really a disappointment. Of course they'll continue to experiment."

"Can you try it on Gerald?"

"Not now. Not with this new infection. Only AIDS patients who have no current infection qualify for the experimental treatment." He stood up to leave.

"But, but Doctor." I couldn't let him go without some kind of hopeful statement—*anything*! "Now that they've isolated the virus, there'll soon be a treatment, won't there? A cure?"

"Soon?" He shook his head wearily. "Not soon. That's a first step. A good step. But I'm afraid it's going to be a long time before it means anything in terms of the patients."

Gerald came home with me after the visit to the clinic to spend the weekend. He was depressed—lower than I'd seen him before.

"Gerald," I said when we were alone after dinner, "I know that medically it looks bleak. But don't give up. Are you still doing your meditations? And writing your affirmations? And doing what your psychotherapist friend tells you to do?"

"David? Yes. We're still working on 'the Monster.'" Gerald and David were delving into Gerald's history, trying to work through negative feelings that Gerald had termed the Monster, a part of him that believed what he'd long been told, that homosexuals were better off dead and that now rose up in triumph to watch the dying. "And I'm still seeing Claire once a week." Gerald thought Claire was wonderful, a woman who had led him through a "rebirthing" process designed to confront and cleanse early wounds and promote healing.

"Do you know what they both told me? Both of them. That I need to get more women in my life. David's gay and Claire's not homophobic, but they both told me that. So much male energy and so little female energy is not good, they said. Claire wants me to have a body massage by a straight woman once a week."

"Really? Heck, I'll give you a massage, Gerald. I'm a straight woman, you know. Lie down."

I arranged Gerald on the floor and worked on the muscles of his shoulders, his back, his legs, and his arms. I looked at my hands kneading his body. They were small hands, good woman's hands. They were strong and filled with life.

"More female energy, huh?" I said. "Sounds like something out of Genesis. Male and female need each other. I could have told you that, Gerald."

"Blossom?"

I stopped massaging and leaned down to listen.

"Would you hold me for a while? Would you get some of your poems to read to me and just hold me?"

"Sure. Sure I will." Gerald had not asked me to hold him in years. I got a stack of poems he had not yet read and brought them back to the family room. Then I lit the gas log and placed the pillows on the couch. We lay down, arranging our bodies comfortably, our arms around one another. It did not feel strange. It felt good.

As I read the poems, Gerald responded with pleasure. He had always been such a good audience, supporter, and friend. Then I put down the poems, kissed his forehead, and stroked his hair that would not grow.

"Gerald, I love you. You know that, don't you? You've always been one of my favorite people. Always."

"I know. I love you too, Blossom."

"What would have happened if—if you had just *made* yourself stay where you were with us? If you had *just forced* yourself to put your other needs away?"

Gerald thought a moment and then replied. "I would have become increasingly bitter and empty—just like Frank." Frank was an old friend whom Gerald had recently run into. He was a homosexual who married and stayed married and had gained eighty pounds in the last two years and hadn't touched anyone during those two years, not even his wife. "I had to do what I've done. I haven't done it perfectly. I would change a lot if I could, but I had to do it." Had to? All that we had, all that we lost. Could not other choices have brought us to some better destination?

And then Gerald spoke of dying. For the first time in all our conversations, he spoke of the very real possibility of death.

"I'm not giving up. I'll continue to fight. But I have to admit that maybe there's a big change coming up for me. And that's all it will be, you know, just a big change. I'll still be me without all this baggage I'm carting around." He gestured disdainfully at his body. "Good riddance to this poor old thing. Gerald will just move on and see what the next lesson is all about. A couple of weeks ago I dreamed I was a butterfly breaking out of a chrysalis. I flew, and it was wonderful!"

Gerald had not seen me cry and I didn't want him to now, so I kept his head on my breast and managed to control my voice. "Oh, Gerald, do you think that somebody is in charge of all this? Oh, I hope that *somebody is in charge of all this!*"

"Of course." I could hear Gerald smile. "You know that, Blossom. We're in charge of this together. Somebody—up there, over there, wherever—has got things under control. But we're in charge too, playing out our parts and learning what we can learn and planning the next scene."

We were silent for a while, listening only to the sound of

the fire and the occasional rain against the dark windows.

Then Gerald spoke again. "Blossom? I don't want you to have a funeral, not a real one. If you and the kids want to do a little something, that's fine, but don't do anything big. I'm typing up Emily Dickinson's poems on death for the kids. Make sure they read them. And I'd like my body to be cremated. I saw advertised in a magazine something called Meadow in a Can. It's a couple of quarts of wildflower seeds. I'm going to order one. I'd like my ashes mixed with the wildflower seeds and then planted somewhere. I would like to be part of a meadow."

On John's birthday I took us all to see Marcel Marceau, the pantomimist. Gerald had spent the morning preparing one of his famous feasts for a birthday dinner and was almost too exhausted to stay awake for the performance. Afterward at his apartment I was helping him with some final things in the kitchen.

"Oh, Gerald, you shouldn't have done all this," I said, stirring the hollandaise sauce. "It takes too much out of you."

"Of course I should have," he replied. "It may be the last thing I can do for John. And it's the only thing I can do on food stamps. And it makes me happy. Doing this is the happiest I've been for weeks."

I watched the children exclaim as Gerald put down on the table another of his masterpieces. He was happy. We all bowed our heads as Gerald said the blessing on the food. Tchaikovsky played quietly in the background. Gerald stood to pour the water. His hand shook so that he could barely fill the glasses.

But John had never had such a birthday feast. And Gerald was happy.

Chapter 14

Gerald's parents wanted to come to visit him for a few days. As I knew it would be depressing for them to be in his small apartment in the city, I invited them all to stay in my large house. Besides, the brightness of the children would lift the grimness of the circumstances. Aaron could play his guitar. Emily could sing. Katy could play the piano. John could show off his turtles and his artwork. They could take Grandpa for a walk to the creek and help him for a moment forget that this was probably the last time he would see his eldest son. And I could have Grandma help me make the salad, healing her pain with cutting tomatoes and lettuce and green onions.

When Gerald and his parents came back from a walk by the ocean, I told him that while they were gone I had called the Simonton Cancer Clinic in Texas, an organization known for its pioneering work in treating cancer from a lifestyle-psychological point of view. A therapist told me he was working with AIDS patients and seemed encouraged at the results.

"I'm sending you to Fort Worth for the weekend," I said. "I've already made the reservation."

Gerald came back from Texas exhausted but determined to follow the program they had developed. Most of the things he had been consistently doing—careful eating, a little exercise, meditation, visualization of the body triumphing over the invading enemy. In addition to this they insisted on a time of play each day and on giving attention to one's "life work," whatever the patient felt he came to this earth to do and had been neglecting. Gerald decided to finish preparing for publication a short children's book he had written, *Tanda's Gift,* whose theme was the validity of us all with our individual gifts, even gifts that are different from everybody else's. His good friend Jay was helping with this project. While Gerald's search for a lover had been unfruitful, he had found many good friends like Jay in the gay community.

School got out the middle of June, and I had been planning for months to take the children on a trip to Utah. My brother Don had invited the boys and me to spend four days with him on a river-rafting trip, for which he was one of the boatmen. I didn't want to leave Gerald, but the children needed this time away. They needed a rest from their concerns about their father. They needed the love and support of family and old friends. They believed Gerald would get well, but there was a lot of stress.

"What do you think, Gerald?" I asked. "Should we go? I hate to leave you alone."

"Of course go," he said. "Go and have a good time. I'll be all right. And it will make me happy to know you guys are out on the river. I wish I could be with you. I'll be okay."

"Are you sure you don't want to stay in the house here while we're gone?"

"Actually, I've changed my mind. I would like to stay here. It's so cold in the city. There's sun out here. I can sit in the backyard and be warm. And it's quiet. The city seems so noisy to me now. I can't take the noise. I want to be alone."

Gerald arranged for some friends to come out and spend some time with him, and I arranged for some of my friends to check in with him. Lynn Ann, our friend and helper from Utah days, was now living in Berkeley and promised to call and come out. And Judy, Gerald's old friend from high school, had spent time with him and was ready to help again. And Anne, my Relief Society visiting teaching companion, was alerted.

We left Gerald with a Father's Day/birthday present of a VCR charged at Penney's and all the funny movies we could borrow from friends. He promised to watch them daily and to do his affirmations and everything else on his list.

It was good to get away for a while. And yet Gerald's illness followed me. Financial pressures followed me, too. I had paid Gerald's rent for a month and sent him to Texas and given him money for other things he needed. Now I had no way of making the house payment that would be due in a couple of weeks.

"What I could really use is a short Christmas book," said my publisher at Bookcraft when I dropped in for a visit. "I don't have one for this season."

There was my house payment. I lay in the back of the truck with my two sons and told myself that before we arrived at the river in two hours I had to have a good Christmas story. It had to be heartwarming and have a surprise ending. I said a prayer and went to work. Within an hour *A Stranger for Christmas* fell into place. Sitting by the river the next day, I wrote the outline, and when we came back to Salt Lake I read it to my publisher. "If you want it," I said, "give me a thousand dollar advance today and I'll write it as soon as I get home. If you don't want it, I'll take it over to Deseret Book."

"We want it," he said, and gave me a check.

When we walked in the door after having been gone for three weeks, I knew. I could tell on the phone that Gerald was losing some ground, but I didn't really know until I saw him. Gerald was dying. He sat on the black couch in his blue bathrobe, thin as the old men in rest homes. He had shaved his beard and his white skin looked almost translucent. He was waiting up for us, so excited for our return.

"Hi, you guys!" he beamed as we walked in the door.

"Hi, Gerald!"

Each of the children embraced him and then I did. I sat beside him on the couch with my arm around him as the children recited to him the highlights of the trip—the river rafting, the fishing, Uncle Don's cabin in Idaho. Gerald listened, delighted. As soon as I could, I sent the children up to bed so we could be alone. In a moment I heard the front door open and I knew that Emily had gone out to the porch. I followed her, sat down on the step beside her, and put my arms around her.

"He's dead," she sobbed. "He's already dead. He's not the same."

"You're right, Emily. All we can do now is help him to go. Let's do our best."

Dear Emily. What could I say to her? How could I help her make any kind of sense of all this? How could she bear to lose Gerald? I rocked her in my arms and kissed her.

If I could erase any twenty-four-hour period from my life, it might be the one that followed next. I was up with Gerald four times in the night. He was disoriented and anxious. The next morning he had arranged for Judy to drive him in to San Francisco to take care of some business with his bank. We walked the two blocks from his apartment to the bank. His feet hurt. They were swollen with the tuberculosis and it was hard for him to walk.

"Can't we drive, Gerald? Let's get in Judy's car."

"No. I want to walk."

I held his arm and we walked, slowly. Oh, to see Gerald's vitality reduced to this! I prayed with every step for strength to help him, to do moment by moment what had to be done, to have Christ on the other side of me. At the bank I told Gerald I was closing out the account and he agreed. He could no longer write, so he put his *X* for the forty-three-dollar check.

Back in Judy's car, I persuaded him to go by the hospital to see if maybe another blood transfusion would be in order. I had called earlier and had been told that if I felt it necessary, I could bring him to emergency. There was none of the caring here that was evidenced on the AIDS ward. This was big-city emergency-room business like you see in the worst movies. I checked Gerald in and he was put on a rolling table and placed behind a small partition. I stayed with him, talking to him and rubbing his head, which seemed to give him some physical and emotional relief from the huge distress he was in. An aide ordered me out. No one but patients are allowed in the room, I was told. I left, and in a few minutes sneaked back in. Gerald needed me. Who was I hurting to stand there and rub his head and hold his hand? Again I was ordered out. I went into the waiting room and cried in Judy's arms for a few minutes. At last they admitted him and came to get me. Yes, a blood transfusion was in order. We could accompany him to 5-B. It was a relief to reach the AIDS ward. If there was anything, anything to be done, they would do it.

Gerald telephoned me the next day. The blood transfusion had given him a boost and he was thinking better.

"Are you watching the news, Blossom? Geraldine Ferraro won the vice-presidential nomination. Isn't that great? What a good step forward."

"Actually, Gerald, I haven't had time to even think about it. I'm sort of swamped with everything else."

"Well, *take* the time. Celebrate a little!"

Celebrate. Gerald was dying and still he could celebrate.

"Gerald? What does the doctor say today?"

"He's releasing me tomorrow. A blood transfusion is all they can do. And they need the bed."

Tomorrow. I had wanted more time. I had wanted to organize the children and the house and set up the guest room properly.

"Blossom?" Gerald had asked me over the phone while we were still away. "When you come back, can I still stay here? Can I stay with you—permanently? I can't go back to the city. I want to be here with you."

"Of course you can, Gerald," I had said. "Of course you can."

I had asked the children what they thought of Gerald's coming home either to get better or to die with us. Of course they wanted him there. How long would it be, I wondered. Dr. Abrams had happened to be on the floor yesterday when Gerald arrived, so I had talked with him. He felt that Gerald could have days left or months; it was hard to say. The social worker had said that there was a facility where AIDS patients could stay for a longer period of time, Garden Sullivan Hospital.

"No," I had said, "I'll take him home."

My good friend Margy called from Hollister and invited the children to stay for a week. I could get everything running on a schedule. Time alone with Gerald would be good. Emily was reluctant to go, but I promised her it would be only for a week.

Dustin, an old friend from BYU, had offered to drive me in to pick up Gerald. Help seemed to have a way of materializing almost miraculously.

A young aide pushed Gerald's wheelchair into the elevator and said brightly, "Going home, huh?"

"Yep." Gerald smiled.

"Home," the aide repeated. "That's a great word, isn't it?"

"It sure is," said Gerald.

As we waited for Dustin to pull up in his van, I spoke further to the young aide.

"I'm just a volunteer," he said. "A few months ago I started coming once a week because I figured they needed help up there. I'd run for this and run for that. Get things for the doctors and the patients. I came more and more and they didn't tell me to go away. So I decided to take a year out of school and just do this. I figure it's the least I can do. And it feels good to help. It sure does feel good to help."

When we arrived home, there was some potato soup left by Charlene, a friend in the ward. The ward. I'd have to let them know what was going on. Word would spread that Gerald was with me, and I wanted the story to be open and clear. I'd go speak to the bishop tomorrow at church. I could leave Gerald long enough to give my Relief Society lesson and speak to the bishop.

"This is very good soup," said Gerald from the couch. "It tastes great."

"Would you like some more?"

"Sure. Blossom? I started taking the medicine in the hospital."

"Medicine?"

"The medicine Dr. Abrams told us about for the tuberculosis. He didn't push it because most of the time it makes the patient really sick. But once in a while it seems to halt the spread of the tuberculosis. I started taking it yesterday."

"How do you feel?"

"Okay. I'm taking it and thinking positive like I did with the pneumonia. Remember how I beat the pneumonia?"

"You did, Gerald. You sure did." I pulled up the little wooden rocker and sat close to him. "All right, kid, listen. We're not giving up. Please don't give up, Gerald. Here. I'm writing down your daily schedule. We're going to get organized and work in earnest. Pills. Humor treatment. Play a game. Listen to the visualization tape. One half-hour meditation. A little exercise. A nap. Anything else?"

"The newspaper. I want to read the newspaper every day."

"Okay. Newspaper. You need a nap now, Gerald. But first we're going to play a game. I brought down the old deck of Authors. Remember our old games of Authors? Now, don't forget that Huckleberry Finn is missing, so Mark Twain only gets three. Okay, four for you. Four for me. I'll go first. Gerald, give me Eight Cousins, by Louisa May Alcott. Gerald?"

He was asleep.

That night Gerald was restless. I could hear him from the couch in the family room, where I was trying to sleep, and went in to be with him.

"Come on, come on!" he had been saying.

"What, Gerald? What?"

"Oh. I was . . . I thought I was in the audience of *La Cage aux Saux,* and I was waiting for the curtain to go up. It wouldn't go up."

A month before, Gerald had purchased a ticket for the show so he'd have something to look forward to. The Broadway musical, a romantic extravaganza, depicted Gerald's dearest dream, a long-term homosexual relationship that really worked. But his ticket was for the night he was in the hospital, and he had asked me to give it to one of his friends.

"Oh, I wanted to see *La Cage,"* he said. "I really wanted to see it."

"Shall I put on the album?" I asked. "I'll do it right now."

I put on the album and turned up the sound so that Gerald could hear it in the guest room. I knelt by the bed and put my head on his chest and wept—for unused theater tickets and unfulfilled dreams.

He dozed off for a little, and then became agitated again.

"Gerald? Let me read you something. Let me get your Walt Whitman book. Would you like to hear some poems?"

"Yes. Yes, I would."

I picked up the worn paperback book that was on the shelf along with the notebooks for writing the daily affirmations. I opened the volume where the marker was and began to read.

> Was someone asking to see the soul?
> See, your own shape and countenance, per-
>   sons, substances, beasts, the trees, the
>   running rivers, the rocks and sands.
> All hold spiritual joys and afterwards loosen
>   them;
> How can the real body ever die and be buried?
>
> Of your real body and any man's or woman's
>   real body,
> Item for item it will elude the hands of
>   the corpse-cleaners and pass to fitting
>   spheres,
> Carrying what has accrued to it from the
>   moment of birth to the moment of death.
>
> Not the types set up by the printer return
>   their impression, the meaning, the main
>   concern,
> Any more than a man's substance and life or a
>   woman's substance and life return in the
>   body and the soul,
> Indifferently before death and after death.
>
> Behold, the body includes and is the meaning,
>   the main concern, and includes and is the
>   soul;
> Whoever you are, how superb and how divine
>   is your body or any part of it!

I stopped reading and looked at Gerald's face, eyes closed, transfixed, intent.

"That's wonderful," he said. "I love that poem."

We slept only a little, and the next morning when Molly called and asked if I would like her to teach my Relief Society lesson, I was grateful. Molly was one of the few who knew what was happening.

"Oh, thanks, Molly. I thought I could, but I only slept a couple of hours last night, and I don't think I should leave Gerald at all today."

I hung up the phone, and then called my visiting teaching companion. "Anne? I can't come to church today. Will you please go in and tell the bishop and his counselors everything? I want them to know."

"Sure. Call you this afternoon."

Oh, my. What a stir this would make through the ward. How would they respond, these righteous Mormon folk who wouldn't even drink a cup of coffee? Would it be just too bizarre for them to deal with? Would we all suddenly become lepers?

"How'd they take it?" I asked when Anne called back that afternoon.

"Fine," she said. "I was amazed. In fact, they told me this isn't their first experience in having to deal with this. Last year a young man moved into the ward boundaries, and when they went to visit him he told them he was gay and would not be participating and wanted to be left alone. But they checked on him every once in a while, and when they learned that he was in the hospital in Oakland they went to see him. He has AIDS. The bishop's been over several times, and the guy's mother is here from Utah. The Elder's Quorum is driving her back and forth from Walnut Greek to the hospital."

I felt tears stinging at my eyes. Well, of course that's

what they would do. People who won't even drink coffee have a hard time understanding homosexuality and AIDS, but they don't have a hard time understanding suffering and need. Mormons have been trained to deal with disaster since pioneer days. They can mobilize a hundred wards to get out the sand bags against a flood in half an hour. And where other floods happen, private floods that leave you adrift, they can get there in a hurry too.

And so I was not surprised to see my Relief Society president at my door first thing the next morning. And with a loaf of bread. Still warm. Oh, that marvelous, proverbial, magically appearing loaf of fresh, warm bread. That symbol of leaven, lifting, and love.

"Hi, Nola Myrl," I said, dissolving into tears. I had never been able to see caring extended without crying. She put her arms around me and cried with me.

"Oh, I didn't know," she said. "I didn't know. I could not imagine how Gerald could leave this beautiful family. I knew nothing. Now I understand. How can we help? Your visiting teacher will be calling today. Let her do everything she can. What else? Do you have a nurse coming in?"

"There's one coming tomorrow for an hour. The hospital arranged it through Public Health."

"What else? Food? Shopping? Anything."

"Well," I said hesitantly, "the backyard is such a mess. I've been gone. Maybe there's a boy in the ward—"

"We'll take care of it."

An hour later my visiting teacher called. "Good morning!" I could tell Sister Spencer's voice anywhere. It was the voice of one who had mastered the art of good cheer even in the midst of the earthquake. She always smiled. Even when she cried she smiled. "Now, I'm not going to say 'let me know if you need something.' That's not good enough. I'm going to call you every morning at nine o'clock and I want you to have your list ready of things you'd like to have done that day. Put a notebook out right now and a pencil and every time something occurs to you, say to yourself, 'I'll have Sister Spencer take care of that,' and you go write it down. Do you understand?"

There was a little potato soup left and Gerald finished it off with a slice of Nola Myrl's good bread. "I'm not sick yet," he said. "I've been on the medicine for four days now and it hasn't made me sick yet."

"Good for you, Gerald."

Again that night he could not calm himself. My body screamed for sleep. I had spent three days alone in unfamiliar territory—changing and washing sheets and bedclothes, finding large enough diapers, putting on and taking off the plastic gloves they had given me in the hospital for protection, counting out vitamin pills—which ones went down once a day and which two times or three—giving Gerald the vile-smelling brown tablets for the tuberculosis, making necessary phone calls. I had not even unpacked from my trip to Utah.

"Gerald, let me sing you a lullaby," I said. I brought in the guitar and the wooden rocker. "Remember this? The one I wrote for Emily . . . 'You came from a land where all is light, to a world half day, a world half night . . .'"

Gerald slept a little, and then awoke in terrible distress. He was having nightmares. "Oh, Blossom, I want to be in the country. I want to be north of the river."

"Gerald? Can I lie down with you for a while? I'll just climb in right here." I placed my body alongside his in the little single bed with my back touching the wall. I drew my knees up inside his, the way we used to sleep years before, and pressed my body as close against his as I could, my arm around his chest. His shaking stopped and he breathed more easily.

"That's good," he said, "Oh, that's good."

He slept. I could not. *Oh, dear God, cut short this horror,* I prayed. *Take Gerald soon. I gave him back to thee six years ago and now I give him back to thee again. Please take him soon. Please take him without pain and agony. Gerald is so dear and so good. Please take him soon.*

In a few minutes Gerald became sick, violently sick. The vile smell of the tuberculosis tablets filled the room as he retched again and again.

It was early morning when I finished cleaning everything up.

"Gerald," I said, "I can't do this alone. Even with a public health nurse coming a couple of times a week, I can't do it alone. I'm going to call your mother. She's trained as a nurse's aide. I think she would come." I made the phone call and then came back. "She'll be here tonight, Gerald. That will be good, to see your mother, won't it?"

"Yes." He was almost too weak to talk.

"Can you eat something, Gerald?"

He shook his head.

"Some carrot juice? Please have some carrot juice."

A chiropractor Gerald had seen had insisted that an immune system can be rebuilt with proper nutrition. He was recommending a diet of pure carrot juice. I had my doubts, but I had borrowed Jo Ellen's juicer and had bought fifty pounds of carrots at the produce store, and I was making Gerald drink all he could.

As I went into the kitchen to make more carrot juice, I heard chopping in the backyard. Probably Nola Myrl had found a boy to do a little weeding. I looked out the window. Well, there was Nola Myrl herself. And there was her husband, Ted, our former bishop who had invited us waterskiing. And their son Todd. All three were out there with their gloves and their hoes and a wheelbarrow, attacking the monster that was my backyard. Without a word, they had just gone to work. I stood for a moment and watched them, tears running down my cheeks. If there were no takers, there could be no givers. I had been a giver before and I would be a giver again. It was my turn to be a taker and I was glad to do it. In a moment, when I could control my face and my voice, I would go out and thank them.

For five hours they worked in the hot July sun. One thing led to another and they couldn't, wouldn't quit. I made carrot juice for Gerald and lemonade for the angels in my backyard and cried over both. When they were through, the lot was as clear as the day I bought it, and the angels left as quietly as they had come.

Gerald's mother arrived and I was glad not to be alone. She was efficient and strong and simply did what had to be done. Her own bewilderment and pain were put away like useless clothing in the back of the closet. She was nurse and mother.

"Hi, Jerry," she said as she arrived, kissing him on the cheek.

He opened his eyes. "Oh, hi, Mom."

Years ago I had had dreams of Gerald's death. We were in the hospital. I was holding one hand and a handsome young man was holding the other. Gerald would have liked that. His man and his woman. But the dream was gone. There was mother and there was wife.

Three days later I knelt by the black leather couch in the front room feeling Gerald's skin become colder and colder. I had stopped making him drink carrot juice and was just giving him a little water now and then from a baby bottle. I had done every final thing I could think of. I had kept Tchaikovsky and Beethoven playing quietly and constantly in the background. I had telephoned Jay and Bill and Claire to come out for a final visit and had picked them up and taken them back to the BART station. "He's in a good place," Claire had said. "I've never felt more love than

I felt in your home." I had held the telephone to Gerald's ear while Emily told him goodbye. I had decided not to send for the children, and Emily—good, brave Emily—wanted to speak to her father even though she knew he couldn't speak back. I couldn't hear what she was saying. But I heard some "thank yous" and I heard "Goodbye, I love you."

I had received cards and flowers and food from friends and people in the ward I hardly knew. Bishop Anderson and my stake president had called, and my home teacher, Brother Sutton, had repaired the shelves in the garage so I could receive Gerald's things. I had spoken to Gerald often, even when he couldn't speak back.

Yesterday morning I had said, "Hi, Gerald."

He had opened his eyes and smiled. "Hi, Blossom."

"I love you, Gerald," I had said.

"I love you too, Blossom." Those were the last words he said.

From then on, I had knelt by the couch every hour or so and spoken to him like he had spoken to me while I was in labor. He had held my legs and told me I was doing fine and that it would soon be over. And now I said the same thing to him in this final labor. "You're doing fine, Gerald," I would say, "You're doing just great. You're almost there."

I had brought down from my bedroom some good-smelling oil and rubbed it on his face and shoulders and arms. "You can go any time you want to go. I will be fine. The kids will be fine. We love you, Gerald."

At one-thirty in the afternoon on July 19, Gerald stopped breathing. I was holding his hand. "You can fly now, Gerald," I said. "Oh, Gerald, now you can fly!"

Epilogue

There is peace. There have been tears and holding and missing. But there is peace.

To help us bring the experience to a conclusion, I conducted a memorial service in our home for the children and a few friends. I led them in a guided meditation, based on the many near-death experiences we had read together for years.

"I want you all to try to participate in what Gerald has just experienced," I said. "Close your eyes. Visualize Gerald, as you knew him when he was in the best of health and vitality. Now see him weaken. You know he is not well. You know he cannot stay long in his body. Lay him down. Watch as his spirit separates itself from his body. He is relieved to be out of that confining, painful place. See him drawn through the dark tunnel, pulled toward the light. He gets closer and closer and emerges in a place of great beauty and peace. He is drawn toward a wonderful being, a Being of Light. The Being receives him with complete love, complete understanding, and reviews with him his life and all that he has learned. Before Gerald moves on with the Being of Light to a place we cannot see, he stops and turns to look at you. He listens as you say to him whatever it is that you feel may have gone unsaid, or that you would like to say one last time. When you're through speaking, you listen. You listen as Gerald speaks to you, telling you some important thing he would like you to remember. You wave him on now and he waves back. You see that he is excited to move on into further life and learning. This is the picture you will hold with you as you think about Gerald."

I then said a prayer, commending Gerald to our Father and Mother in Heaven.

To conclude the service I gave each person a new candle and had them light it from a candle I had brought from Gerald's apartment. "I want you to consider light for a moment now," I said. "Gerald's light. Your own light. Let us resolve to find ways to make it brighter."

I watch the children leap again into life and I am unendingly grateful. "I don't worry about the children," Gerald had said to me more than once. "Each of them is so strong, so good."

I hear the children running old home movies downstairs and hear Gerald's voice and wonder how they are handling it. Emily runs upstairs in a few moments, exclaiming, "Oh, it was so good to hear Gerald singing 'Happy Birthday'!"

We sit together and watch the video of "We Are the World," designed to raise money for the starving Africans. It finishes and John sits quietly for a moment and then says, "This is something Gerald would like."

We celebrate one of the children's birthdays, and bring out the bottles of bubble-blowing solution. After a few minutes one of the children says, "I'm going to go blow bubbles to Gerald!" All four race out to the backyard and stand on the Ping-Pong table and the balcony and happily blow bubbles to Gerald, as high and as bright as they can.

I look at the calendar for the month of July and see that hearts and messages of love have been drawn on the dates of his birth and of his death.

Life with its inexorable currents moves me with it. I can think and speak and write of Gerald with peace. Only now and then, when I hear a particular melody or catch a certain phrase, do I have to stop what I'm doing and lean against something for a moment. Sometimes I read and have no answer for the question I found on a card when I cleared off Gerald's desk, a quotation from Hermann Hesse: "I wanted only to try to live in accord with the promptings which came from my true self. Why was that so very difficult?"

Gerald's friends in the chorus held a service for him. They invited me, but I did not attend. I had said my good-byes in my own way on my own territory, and I couldn't bear to do it again on Castro Street. They had a fine informal service. They sang Gerald's song and read his poems and reminded one another of his vision. On the day of the winter solstice Jay took Gerald's ashes, loaded with wild-flower seeds, up to Mount Tamalpais. By now I'm sure that Gerald has made a meadow.

Gerald and I will have our picnic. I'm planning it now. Our many picnics. After I have traveled the tunnel and been welcomed into the light, I will search the faces for one of my favorite people, and he will be there. Gerald and I will walk together and laugh and embrace, sealed as friends forever through years of tears and hopes and joys and devastation and the final, precious knowledge of how dearly we still loved each other after all the weeping was done.

And Whoever is in charge of all this will walk with us, and will help us to sort out the mysteries and help us to complete the healing. Walls will fall and we will see each other more clearly—all of us, the Mormons and the

Catholics and the Jews and the Muslims and the straights and the gays and the women and the men. Confusions will lift like fog lifts from the Golden Gate Bridge on a good summer day, and we will each see our next step and will take it.

Gerald's insatiable hunger for learning will find ready fields. And I will smile as I see him bounding in with some bright new knowledge to share, very much as I saw him bounding up the stairs hundreds of times, his blond head a rising sun. "Blossom, did you know . . . ?"

Additional Works by the Author

Ms. Pearson has again addressed the subject of homosexuality in a new book, *No More Goodbyes: Circling the Wagons Around Our Gay Loved Ones*, available at www. nomoregoodbyes.com.

Her stage play, *Facing East*, tells the story of a Mormon couple dealing with the suicide of their gay son. To purchase the book or DVD or to learn about current productions or production rights, see www.nomoregoodbyes.com/facing-east.